REA: THE TEST PREP AP® TEACHERS RECOMMEND

2nd Edition

AP® ENGLISH LITERATURE AND COMPOSITION
CRASH COURSE®

By Dawn Hogue, M.A.

WITHDRAWN

Research & Education Association

Visit our website at: www.rea.com

Research & Education Association
258 Prospect Plains Road
Cranbury, New Jersey 08512
Email: info@rea.com

AP® ENGLISH LITERATURE AND COMPOSITION CRASH COURSE®, 2nd Edition

Printed in the United States of America

Library of Congress Control Number 2019939455

ISBN-13: 978-0-7386-1257-7
ISBN-10: 0-7386-1257-X

REA Crash Course® and REA® are registered trademarks of Research & Education Association, Inc.

AP ENGLISH LITERATURE AND COMPOSITION CRASH COURSE
TABLE of CONTENTS

ABOUT OUR BOOK

REA's *AP English Literature and Composition Crash Course* is designed for the last-minute studier or any student who wants a quick refresher on the AP course. The *Crash Course* is based on the latest 2019–2020 changes to the AP English Literature and Composition course and exam and focuses only on the skills and topics tested, so you can make the most of your study time.

Written by a veteran AP English Literature and Composition test expert, our *Crash Course* gives you a concise review of the major concepts and important topics tested on the AP English Literature and Composition exam.

- **Part I** offers you **Keys for Success**, so you can tackle the exam with confidence. It also gives you strategies to help build your overall point score.

- **Part II** is an overview of the **basic elements of literature**. The chapters focus on fiction, poetry, and language, and provide a handy summary of literary periods, authors, and concepts.

- **Part III** covers **how to interpret reading passages** and explains literary themes.

- **Part IV** is devoted exclusively to essay writing, offering a **review of essay basics** and an in-depth analysis of an essay prompt to help improve your composition skills.

- **Part V** gives you expert advice on **how to master the multiple-choice section** of the exam. Test-taking strategies and practice test questions help ensure you're ready for test day.

ABOUT OUR ONLINE PRACTICE EXAM

How ready are you for the AP English Literature and Composition exam? Find out by taking **REA's online practice exam** available at *www.rea.com/ studycenter*. This test features automatic scoring, detailed explanations of all answers, and diagnostic score reporting that will help you identify your strengths and weaknesses.

Whether you use this book throughout the school year or as a refresher in the final weeks before the exam, REA's *Crash Course* will show you how to study efficiently and strategically, so you can boost your score.

Good luck on your AP English Literature and Composition exam!

ABOUT OUR AUTHOR

Dawn Hogue taught all levels of high school English and AP English for the Sheboygan Falls School District, Sheboygan Falls, Wisconsin. She has earned numerous awards and recognition for her role in the classroom.

Ms. Hogue received her B.A. in English, graduating summa cum laude, from Lakeland University, Sheboygan, Wisconsin. She also earned her M.A. in Education from Lakeland University and her M.S. in Educational Leadership from Cardinal Stritch University, Milwaukee.

She is interested in promoting technology and web resources in the classroom and maintains a website (*www.mshogue.com*) for that purpose. Ms. Hogue was an adjunct faculty member at Johns Hopkins University's Center for Talented Youth, where she worked in digital spaces to help gifted students improve their writing skills.

Ms. Hogue is also the author of REA's *AP English Language and Composition Crash Course*.

ABOUT REA

Founded in 1959, Research & Education Association (REA) is dedicated to publishing the finest and most effective educational materials—including study guides and test preps—for students of all ages.

Today, REA's wide-ranging catalog is a leading resource for students, teachers, and other professionals. Visit *www.rea.com* to see a complete listing of all our titles.

ACKNOWLEDGMENTS

We would like to thank Larry B. Kling, Editorial Director, for his overall direction; Pam Weston, Publisher, for setting the quality standards for production integrity and managing the publication to completion; John Cording, Technology Director, for managing the REA Study Center; Diane Goldschmidt, Managing Editor, and Wayne Barr, Test Prep Project Manager, for shepherding this book through development and production; Alice Leonard, Senior Editor, for editorial review; and Jennifer Calhoun for file prep.

We also extend our appreciation to Kathy Caratozzolo of Caragraphics for typesetting.

PART I:

INTRODUCTION

Keys for Success
on the AP English Literature and Composition Exam

It was July 1995, after my first year teaching AP English. My son had taken a phone message from one of my students who was very excited to tell me the results of her exam. He said, "Mom, one of your students called and said she got a 4 on some test." Confused by what appeared to be a very low score, he then asked, "Is that good?" I smiled. Not good. It is great!

OVERVIEW

The Odyssey by Homer is considered the first epic poem. The first English novel is often said to be *Robinson Crusoe* by Daniel Defoe written in 1719. Walt Whitman, who lived and wrote in the 1800s, is said to be the father of free verse. There is a long, complex history of world literature, and there is so much to know. Even college literature professors do not study the entirety of the literary field but instead specialize in a particular aspect, such as British Romanticism. You are not expected to know it all, either. How could you?

The AP English Literature and Composition Exam presents many challenges, and even if you had read every book ever written, you might not be prepared for what is in store for you. So, knowing that you can't study it all, the purpose of this book is to give you the most important keys to success.

In the chapters that follow, you will get content-specific help, tips for success, and general insight about what you need to know.

BIG IDEAS AND ENDURING UNDERSTANDINGS

In 2019, the College Board organized its new course framework around what they call "Big Ideas and Enduring Understandings."

The "big ideas" are divided into six areas you should already be familiar with:

- Character
- Setting
- Structure
- Narration
- Figurative Language
- Literary Argumentation

The AP English Literature and Composition exam will test all six of these big ideas. To oversimplify and think that you need only to know the definitions of the terms above would be a tremendous error.

An "enduring understanding" is a concept a bit harder to explain, but basically, "enduring understanding" encompasses your knowledge and your skills, or what you know and what you can do with what you know, particularly after emerging from a higher-level English course, an Advanced Placement course in particular.

In many ways, the College Board's new course framework is geared toward your teachers to guide them in planning your AP course. But this book is written particularly for you and can be viewed as a direct complement to your in-school coursework. However, if you are not enrolled in an AP English Literature course, this book is even more vital to your success.

STRUCTURE OF THE EXAM

The AP English Literature and Composition exam is given each May and is approximately 3 hours long.

Part I consists of approximately 55 multiple-choice questions to be answered in 60 minutes. Each question has five answer choices. Part I counts for 45 percent of your total exam score.

Part II of the exam requires you to answer 3 free-response questions that count for 55% of your total exam score. Two hours is allowed for answering the free-response questions.

Test proctors will give a ten-minute break between Part I and Part II. (Your AP English Literature and Composition instructor is not allowed to proctor your exam.)

AP English Lit Units	Exam Weighting
Short Fiction (Units 1, 4, 7)	42%–49%
Poetry (Units 2, 5, 8)	36%–45%
Longer Fiction or Drama (Units 3, 6, 9)	15%–18%

Source: College Board, Fall 2019 AP English Literature and Composition Course and Exam Description

The table above tells you a great deal at a glance. For example, it may seem like you should read a lot of short stories since short fiction is weighted so heavily. But that's not exactly right. Instead, realize that shorter works make it easier for students to comprehend the function of literary elements. Thus, your teacher is likely to use short works as a teaching tool more often. This does not mean longer fiction and drama are less valuable genres to study or that you should spend less time on them. In fact, balancing your reading to include all genres is a vital aspect of preparing for this exam. As you will learn later, question no. 3 in the free-response section expects you to have in-depth experience with at least a few longer works. Also, be mindful that poetry plays a bigger role on the exam than you may have expected—its weighted value could be up to 45% of your exam.

SCORING THE EXAM

The multiple-choice section of the exam is scored by machine. Scores on the multiple-choice section are based only on the number of questions answered correctly. Points are not deducted for incorrect answers and no points are awarded for unanswered questions. It is to your advantage to answer every multiple-choice question. If you do not know the answer, try to eliminate as many choices as you can and then select the best answer from the remaining choices.

The three essays are scored by AP readers in early June. Readers include college professors and experienced AP English teachers, who meet for this purpose. These readers score essays using scoring rubrics created by the College Board's test development committee for this exam. Your essay is not identified by name or geographical location. Every effort is made to ensure objectivity and fairness in assessing essays.

The scores from Part I and Part II are combined to create a composite score. Scores are reported to students and designated colleges in July.

AP SCORE SCALE

The College Board uses a formula (which changes slightly from year to year) to rank your combined multiple-choice and free-response scores into five categories:

5 = Extremely Well Qualified
4 = Well Qualified
3 = Qualified
2 = Possibly Qualified
1 = No Recommendation

Qualification means you may receive college credit or advanced placement at colleges and universities in the United States and Canada. In their information to students, the College Board writes that, "You may be very surprised to see that your composite score can be approximately two-thirds of the total possible score and you could still earn a grade of 5!" Earning that score on other exams might translate to an "F" at worst and a "D" at best. In other words, you do not have to get all the multiple-choice questions correct or write perfect essays to get a high score on the exam.

In the 2017 figures reported by the College Board, approximately 53% of all students who took the exam scored a 3 or higher. And while fewer than 10% of students scored a 5 (which says a bit about the difficulty of the exam), you should focus on the high number who earned a qualifying score.

WHAT TO KNOW ABOUT EXAM DAY

What you can (should have) and cannot have in the exam room:

Yes	No
Several no. 2 pencils, sharpened, with good erasers	Cell phones, mp3 players, or any other electronic device, including calculators
One or two reliable blue or black pens; avoid pens that clump or bleed	Cameras or other recording devices
A noiseless watch (with no internet access), so you can monitor your time	Books, including dictionaries
Your Social Security number	Scratch paper
Water (No bottles with paper labels are allowed.)	Notes you've made in advance
	Highlighters

Preparing yourself personally:

1. Eat well in the weeks prior to the exam. Get used to eating breakfast, so that you can eat a good breakfast on exam day consisting of fruit, lean protein, and complex carbohydrates. Also, drink water, not sugared drinks.

2. Get your sleep and not just the night before the exam. Establish good sleep patterns in the weeks prior to the exam. Teens typically do not get enough sleep. Aim for 8–9 hours a night.

3. Wake up early enough to be fully awake and ready to go on exam day. Set your alarm so you don't oversleep. You don't want to be groggy.

4. Caffeine or energy drinks may help you to be more alert, but overdoing them can make you jittery and make it harder for you to focus. If you are not used to caffeine, avoid it on exam day.

5. Wear comfortable clothes and shoes on the day of the exam. Prepare for fluctuations in room temperature by wearing layers that you can adjust.

See more in Chapter 2 about what you can do to prepare for exam day.

Test Tip

Don't take my word for it. Research the effect of health and wellness on academic performance. You'll enhance your informed and active reading skills by doing this research.

Student Tools:
What You Bring
to Your Own Success

OVERVIEW

Any study text is useless if you don't pair it with your best intentions. This brief chapter simply outlines what you can do to enhance your own success.

A STATE OF MIND: THE THREE D'S

DESIRE:

This book can only help so much. You have to want to be successful. Your desire to do well must translate into your determination and diligence. But also, your desire must be coupled with a positive and energetic attitude. You have chosen this task because you desire to push yourself. It won't be easy, but most things worthy of our time are not easy.

DETERMINATION:

Whether you are using this book on its own or along with a structured AP English Literature course, you have a lot to accomplish. No book or teacher can do for you what you need to do for yourself. You must be resolute in your determination to accomplish your goals.

DILIGENCE:

You have to keep at it, even when things get tough.

Test Tip

Make a bracelet to wear that displays the three D's to remind you how important your state of mind is. If you ever feel like slacking, your bracelet can remind you to put forth your best effort.

A MATTER OF TIME

You may have heard the saying, "What's worth doing, is worth doing well." This is also true for your preparation for the AP Lit exam—it's worth doing well! It will be very difficult for you to literally cram all you need to know into a short period of time. The information and tips you get in this book will help you to focus and prepare for your exam. However, it is best if you start early enough to really learn what you need to know and practice essential skills. Except for some literary terms and methods and strategies, there is little in this text that you can actually memorize. Instead, you need to develop your reading, writing, and thinking skills.

SUGGESTED STRATEGIES FOR USING THIS BOOK

1. Read the entire book, noting which topics or chapters will require the most study time. Focus on what you need to know instead of what you already know.

2. You'll notice strategic repetition in some areas in this book, where a term or a concept is defined or

explained again, perhaps in a slightly different context or different words or perhaps for a different purpose. Instead of thinking, *Wait, I've read this already*, go ahead and read it again. It's been said that the human brain needs to hear something seven times for it to stick for good. Whether or not that notion is true for you, it never hurts to reiterate important concepts.

3. Make a goal sheet, listing specific tasks for the upcoming months. For example,

   • Read three novels and two plays and fill out a *Remembering Major Works* form for each one (see Chapter 4).

   • Practice your critical reading skills by annotating all the texts you read.

4. Good goals have time limits, so be sure to say when you plan to meet your goals.

5. Re-read this book or sections of it as often as necessary to reinforce ideas. Most people will not remember everything they read the first time.

6. Make a short list of the five most important skills you need to improve before test time, such as *reading complex texts* or *understanding figurative language*. Find ways to practice those skills.

7. Form an AP Lit study team with friends who will be taking the exam. Learn from each other. Here are some reasons to form a study team:

   • Team members can quiz each other on subject terms.

   • Members can share essays to review them. Peer review can help team members to see strengths and weaknesses in their writing. They can also learn from the reading of each other's work.

   • Members who choose to read the same books, can discuss them, which helps everyone to understand a text more deeply.

8. If you get frustrated, try these strategies:

- Analyze the reason for your frustration. Why are you frustrated? What can you do to alleviate your frustration?
- Take a short break to refocus: go for a walk outdoors, with no headphones. Let nature (or the city) help you get out of yourself for a while.
- Talk to your study group and vent. Then, together, find ways to get back on track.
- Ask your teacher for help.

MORE TIPS

- As crazy as it sounds in this digital age, handwriting counts: not everyone has good handwriting, but in preparation for the exam, you should do as much as you can to improve yours. If you do not write legibly on your essays, you are jeopardizing your score. You cannot expect tired, overworked AP readers to struggle with your essay needlessly. When you write your practice essays, always use blue or black ink and always write with an imagined reader in mind.
- This exam is about scholarship. You should think of yourself as you embark on this "quest" as an upper-level scholar—a college student, really. If you wear the garb of scholar, even metaphorically, it will influence how you think about things.
- Your attitude is more important than you think—it influences everything, even your physical well-being. A positive attitude will give you energy and confidence. A negative attitude will
  - limit your ability to read carefully (you'll want to rush, skim, get it over with)
  - lead to frustration and fatigue
  - keep you from having an open mind
  - possibly infect others, giving them doubt about their own abilities

- You need to study hard and take the exam seriously, but also realize that it is just one test of what you know—at one point in your life. This exam is not the most important thing you will ever do. Try to keep it all in perspective.

Make Flash Cards: use 3 x 5 index cards to write out terms or concepts to memorize and review. Recent studies show that the act of writing notes by hand can improve memory retention better than using a digital device. Another advantage is that a packet of index cards is portable—you can quiz yourself while you wait for the dentist.

PART II:

ELEMENTS OF LITERATURE AND MORE

Summary of Literature and Representative Authors

OVERVIEW

Literature might be thought of as the creative measure of history. Great writers, poets, and playwrights weave their sense of life and the events of their time (their own histories) into works of art. It seems impossible to disconnect most literary works from their historical context, but the themes that make their work universal and enduring perhaps do transcend time in that they speak to people of all time, ensuring us that we are all part of something much larger than simply the here and now.

When you review the literary concepts that follow and study the timeline, you will see that shifts in literary theory or tradition are often precipitated by major events in history, most notably wars. The ways that history is linked to literature are endless, and this chapter only hints at some of them.

The information in this chapter is not here for you to memorize. In fact there are rarely questions on the exam that expect you to know particular literary periods and their characteristics. However, it will not hurt you to have a sense of how literature (particularly

Western literature) has evolved over time. Additionally, this timeline and the representative authors should help you determine a reading list for your study.

A FEW MAJOR CONCEPTS OR "ISMS"

The following list is given in chronological order. This list focuses primarily on American literature.

Romanticism (mid-19th century)

- Valued feeling over reason
- Valued the individual, but recognized that individuals often feel alienated
- Literature characterized by elements of the supernatural, appreciation for the beauty of nature, personal introspection

Transcendentalism (mid-19th century)

- An offshoot of American Romanticism led by Bronson Alcott, Henry David Thoreau, and Ralph Waldo Emerson
- Favored self-reliance and non-conformity
- Sought to see the sublime in the ordinary
- Believed that to transcend was to reach beyond ordinary experience—self-perfection was an aim

Realism (mid- to late 19th century)

- Pre– and post–Civil War
- Writers rejected sentimentality, wanted to represent true life experience, including the way people really acted and spoke
- Shunned flowery diction and romanticism
- The rise of the women's movement is also significant.

Regionalism (19th century)

- Extension of Realism
- Focus on local setting, customs, and dialects

Naturalism (19th century)

- Extension of Realism
- Themes are darker: crime, poverty, prejudice, etc.
- Naturalist writers tried to understand scientific or psychological reasons behind human behavior

Imagism (early 20th century)

- Movement in poetry that favored the use of images as the things themselves
- Motto: "The natural object is always the adequate symbol."
- Willingness to play with forms
- Most notable poets: Ezra Pound and William Carlos Williams

The Lost Generation (1914–)

- "The Lost Generation" is the phrase coined by writer Gertrude Stein and later made popular by Ernest Hemingway
- Referred to the generation who lost fathers, husbands, sons and brothers in World War I and who felt aimless and without foundation
- Many of the lost were disillusioned by traditional American values and became expatriates, who chose to leave the United States for Europe, Mexico, and elsewhere. (Paris was an especially favored destination.)

The Harlem Renaissance (1920s)

- The explosion of African American visual art, dance, music, and literature in the 1920s, primarily centered in the upper Manhattan neighborhood of Harlem
- Poet Langston Hughes is often seen as the iconic literary figure of the period.

Modernism (1918–1945)

- The prolific period between the end of World War I and the end of World War II

- Other historical context:
  - ▸ *The Industrial Revolution and the age of machines*
  - ▸ *Mass immigration to the United States*
  - ▸ *Women's rights (19th amendment)*
  - ▸ *The Great Depression*

- Alienation and the loss of the individual to the machine are major themes.

Postmodernism (1945–)

- Begins with detonation of atomic bombs in Japan, ending World War II

- Key markers:
  - ▸ *Post-apocalyptic themes*
  - ▸ *Satire*
  - ▸ *The absurd*
  - ▸ *Anti-heroes*
  - ▸ *The rise of multiculturalism and diverse voices*

- Themes:
  - ▸ *Alienation due to race, gender, and sexual orientation*
  - ▸ *Intolerance*
  - ▸ *Political and social oppression*

The Beat Movement (1950s)

- Led by poet Allen Ginsberg and novelist Jack Kerouac

- Rejected mainstream American values and embraced nonconformity and Eastern philosophy

- The forefather of the 1960s counterculture movement (Hippie Movement)

Gonzo Journalism (1970–)

- Invented by Hunter S. Thompson in 1970

- Refers to a new kind of journalism where the writer often is part of the story, blending fact and fiction

Magical Realism (1960s–)

- Magical or supernatural elements appear in otherwise realistic circumstances
- First considered an element of painting
- Mostly associated with Latin American writers, especially Gabriel Garcia Marquez, Carlos Fuentes, and Isabel Allende

Creative Nonfiction (late 20th and early 21st centuries)

- A genre that blends elements of literature with nonfiction
- Includes memoir, travel and place essays, personal narratives, etc.

LITERARY TIMELINE

Literary timelines are readily available to literature students. The value of a timeline is to show literary works in a historical context and in relationship to other works. The timeline below is not inclusive, but shows some of the major writers of each literary period. Consult Chapter 4 for lists of works commonly cited on the AP Lit exam.

800–400 BCE

World Literature

Greek writers: Homer, *The Iliad* and *The Odyssey*

Sophocles, *Oedipus Rex* and *Antigone*

Euripedes, *Medea*

250 BCE–150 CE

World Literature

Roman writers: Vergil, *The Aeneid*

Horace, poet and satirist

Ovid, lyrical poet

450–1066

World Literature

Haiku poetry in Japan

British Literature (Anglo-Saxon Period)

Beowulf

1066–1500

World Literature

Italian writers: Petrarch: sonnets

Dante Alighieri: *The Divine Comedy*

Boccaccio: *The Decameron*

British Literature (Middle English Period)

Geoffrey Chaucer: *Canterbury Tales*

German Johannes Gutenberg invents the printing press

Gutenberg's moveable type printing press (mid-15th century) is arguably the most significant invention in the history of literature. The printing press not only made the printed word cheaper to produce, but it also brought books out of the cloistered realm of the aristocracy and helped increase literacy among all classes of people.

1500–1660: The Renaissance

World Literature

Miguel de Cervantes, Spanish writer: *Don Quixote*

British Literature

Shakespeare

Christopher Marlowe: *Dr. Faustus*

Ben Jonson, known for satirical plays and lyric poetry

John Donne, known for metaphysical conceits

Edmund Spenser: *The Faerie Queen*

Andrew Marvell: *To His Coy Mistress*

John Milton: *Paradise Lost*

1660–1785: The Neoclassical Period

World Literature

Molière, French, *Tartuffe*

Voltaire, French, *Candide*

Jean-Jacques Rousseau, French writer and philosopher

Johann Wolfgang von Goethe, German writer

British Literature

Alexander Pope, British poet

Daniel Defoe, *Robinson Crusoe* and *Moll Flanders*

Jonathan Swift: *Gulliver's Travels* and *A Modest Proposal*

Samuel Johnson

The rise of the novel

American Literature (Puritan/Colonial Period)

Jonathan Edwards, *Sinners in the Hands of an Angry God* (sermon)

Anne Bradstreet, poet

Puritan writing was God centered, plain in style, instructive in purpose.

1750–1800:

American Literature
(The Age of Reason/Revolutionary Literature)

Thomas Jefferson, Thomas Paine: *Common Sense*

Benjamin Franklin

African-American poet Phillis Wheatley, *Poetry on Various Subjects*

Period recognized by emerging nationalism; characterized by persuasive, philosophical writing: speeches, pamphlets, and the beginnings of newspapers in America.

1785–1830: The Romantic Period/Romanticism

British Literature

William Blake, William Wordsworth

Samuel Taylor Coleridge: *The Rime of the Ancient Mariner*

Jane Austen

Lord Byron

Percy Bysshe Shelley

John Keats

Mary Shelley: *Frankenstein*

American Literature

Washington Irving: *Rip Van Winkle*

William Cullen Bryant: *Thanatopsis*

James Fenimore Cooper: *The Last of the Mohicans*

Nathaniel Hawthorne (often included in this period), see below.

1832–1901: The Victorian Period

World Literature

Henrik Ibsen, Norwegian dramatist: *A Doll's House*

Victor Hugo, French: *Les Misérables*

Gustave Flaubert, French: *Madame Bovary*

British Literature

Robert Browning, poet

Elizabeth Barrett Browning, poet

Charles Dickens: *Great Expectations*

Charlotte Brontë: *Jane Eyre*

Emily Brontë: *Wuthering Heights*

Alfred, Lord Tennyson

William Makepeace Thackeray: *Vanity Fair*

George Eliot, a.k.a. Marian Evans: *Middlemarch*

American Literature

Henry James

Frederick Douglass: *Narrative of the Life of Frederick Douglass, an American Slave*

Harriet Jacobs: *Incidents in the Life of a Slave Girl*

Paul Laurence Dunbar: *Lyrics of a Lowly Life*

1840–1860: American Renaissance

Transcendentalism and American Gothic (dark romantics)

Emily Dickinson, poet

Walt Whitman: *Leaves of Grass*

Nathaniel Hawthorne: *The Scarlet Letter*

Herman Melville: *Moby Dick*

Edgar Allan Poe, poems and short stories

Transcendentalist Writers

Ralph Waldo Emerson, essays and aphorisms

Henry David Thoreau: *Walden*

Bronson Alcott

Margaret Fuller, first major feminist writer

1855–1900: American Realism/Regionalism

Mark Twain (born Samuel Clemens): *The Adventures of Huckleberry Finn*

Bret Harte: regional writer

Stephen Crane: *The Red Badge of Courage*

Kate Chopin: *The Awakening*

Charlotte Perkins Gilman: *The Yellow Wallpaper*

1901–1914

British (Edwardian Period)

Joseph Conrad, Polish/British author: *Heart of Darkness*

American (Naturalism)

Theodore Dreiser, novelist: *Sister Carrie*

W.E.B. Du Bois, sociologist and author: *The Souls of Black Folk*

Jack London, novelist: *The Call of the Wild*

Edith Wharton, novelist: *Ethan Frome*

1919–1945: Modernism

World Literature

Albert Camus, French writer: *The Stranger*

British Literature

George Orwell (born Eric Blair): *Animal Farm* and *1984*

American Literature

John Steinbeck, Nobel Prize novelist: *Of Mice and Men* and *The Grapes of Wrath*

Zora Neale Hurston, novelist: *Their Eyes Were Watching God*

Langston Hughes, poet

Tennessee Williams, playwright: *The Glass Menagerie*

1950– : Postmodernism

British Literature

William Golding, British author: *Lord of the Flies*

American Literature

(Note: Ethnicities are listed below only to show the range of diversity in literature in this period.)

J.D. Salinger, novelist: *The Catcher in the Rye*

Ralph Ellison, African-American novelist: *Invisible Man*

Arthur Miller, playwright: *The Crucible* and *Death of a Salesman*

Ray Bradbury, science fiction writer: *Fahrenheit 451*

Eugene O'Neill, playwright: *Long Day's Journey Into Night*

Jack Kerouac, Beat writer: *On the Road*

Elie Wiesel, Romanian-American writer: *Night*

Joseph Heller, novelist: *Catch 22*

John Knowles, novelist: *A Separate Peace*

Ken Kesey, American author: *One Flew Over the Cuckoo's Nest*

Sylvia Plath, known mostly for poetry (1932–1963): *The Bell Jar*

Chaim Potok, Jewish-American novelist: *The Chosen*

Maya Angelou, African-American author: *I Know Why the Caged Bird Sings*

Toni Morrison, African-American Nobel Prize novelist: *The Bluest Eye*

Rudolfo Anaya, Mexican-American writer: *Bless Me, Ultima*

Maxine Hong Kingston, Asian-American writer: *The Woman Warrior*

Alice Walker, African-American writer: *The Color Purple*

August Wilson, African-American, Pulitzer Prize winning playwright: *Fences* and *The Piano Lesson*

Sandra Cisneros, Hispanic-American writer: *The House on Mango Street*

Louise Erdrich, Native American writer: *Love Medicine*

Amy Tan, Asian-American novelist: *The Joy Luck Club*

REPRESENTATIVE AUTHORS

According to the College Board, "The following authors are provided simply to suggest the range and quality of reading expected in the course." The key wording here is "range and quality of reading expected." Students in AP English Literature courses are expected to read a variety of complex and quality works from British, American, and World authors. What is new as of 2019 is a de-emphasis on pre-20th century literature. This is not to say there won't be passages from Shakespeare or John Donne, for example, but there may be fewer of them.

The next chapter should help you link themes and titles to many of these names and provide you with some ideas for texts to study.

POETRY

W.H. Auden; Elizabeth Bishop; William Blake; Anne Bradstreet; Edward Kamau Brathwaite; Gwendolyn Brooks; Robert Browning; George Gordon, Lord Byron; Lorna Dee Cervantes; Geoffrey Chaucer; Lucille Clifton; Samuel Taylor Coleridge; Billy Collins; H. D. (Hilda Doolittle); Emily Dickinson; John Donne; Rita Dove; Paul Laurence Dunbar; T.S. Eliot; Robert Frost; Joy Harjo; Seamus Heaney; George Herbert; Garrett Hongo; Gerard Manley Hopkins; Langston Hughes; Ben Jonson; John Keats; Philip Larkin; Robert Lowell; Andrew Marvell; John Milton; Marianne Moore; Sylvia Plath; Edgar Allan Poe; Alexander Pope; Adrienne Rich; Anne Sexton; William Shakespeare; Percy Bysshe Shelley; Leslie Marmon Silko; Cathy Song; Wallace Stevens; Alfred, Lord Tennyson; Derek Walcott; Walt Whitman; Richard Wilbur; William Carlos Williams; William Wordsworth; William Butler Yeats

DRAMA

Aeschylus; Edward Albee; Amiri Baraka; Samuel Beckett; Anton Chekhov; Caryl Churchill; William Congreve; Athol Fugard; Lorraine Hansberry; Lillian Hellman; David Henry Hwang; Henrik Ibsen; Ben Jonson; David Mamet; Arthur Miller; Molière; Marsha Norman; Sean O'Casey; Eugene O'Neill; Suzan-Lori Parks; Harold Pinter; Luigi Pirandello; William Shakespeare; George Bernard Shaw; Sam Shepard; Sophocles; Tom Stoppard; Luis Valdez; Oscar Wilde; Tennessee Williams; August Wilson

FICTION (NOVEL AND SHORT STORY)

Chinua Achebe; Sherman Alexie; Isabel Allende; Rudolfo Anaya; Margaret Atwood; Jane Austen; James Baldwin; Saul Bellow; Charlotte Brontë; Emily Brontë; Raymond Carver; Willa Cather; Sandra Cisneros; John Cheever; Kate Chopin; Joseph Conrad; Edwidge Danticat; Daniel Defoe; Anita Desai; Charles Dickens; Fyodor Dostoevsky; George Eliot; Ralph Ellison; Louise Erdrich; William Faulkner; Henry Fielding; F. Scott Fitzgerald; E.M. Forster; Thomas Hardy; Nathaniel Hawthorne; Ernest Hemingway; Zora Neale Hurston; Kazuo Ishiguro; Henry James; Ha Jin; Edward P. Jones; James Joyce; Maxine Hong Kingston; Joy Kogawa; Jhumpa Lahiri; Margaret Laurence; D. H. Lawrence; Chang-rae Lee; Bernard Malamud; Gabriel García Márquez; Cormac McCarthy; Ian McEwan; Herman Melville; Toni Morrison; Bharati Mukherjee; Vladimir Nabokov; Flannery O'Connor; Orhan Pamuk; Katherine Anne Porter; Marilynne Robinson; Jonathan Swift; Mark Twain; John Updike; Alice Walker; Evelyn Waugh; Eudora Welty; Edith Wharton; John Edgar Wideman; Virginia Woolf; Richard Wright

EXPOSITORY PROSE

Joseph Addison; Gloria Anzaldúa; Matthew Arnold; James Baldwin; James Boswell; Jesús Colón; Joan Didion; Frederick Douglass; W.E.B. Du Bois; Ralph Waldo Emerson; William Hazlitt; bell hooks; Samuel Johnson; Charles Lamb; Thomas Macaulay; Mary McCarthy; John Stuart Mill; George Orwell; Michael Pollan; Richard Rodriguez; Edward Said; Lewis Thomas; Henry David Thoreau; E.B. White; Virginia Woolf

Summary of
Literary Texts

OVERVIEW

In combination with the previous chapter, the purpose of this section is to acquaint you with the variety and types of literary works that have been on past exams and may appear on future exams. While you are not expected to have read all of these works—that would be impossible—you are expected to have read a wide variety of works. It is better to know *five to seven* novels/plays very well than to have a cursory knowledge of more literary works.

If you study the first list that follows, you will find that most of the titles are novels or plays. Some short fictional works are listed along with a few (very few) non-fiction texts.

Test Tip

If time is short, focus on reading and studying a few novels and plays. Choose those most often cited on the AP Lit exam if you have no other impulse guiding your decision. See the list below.

Also, if you look at the tags for the most prominently cited works, you'll see some common denominators, which may indicate the types of themes the College Board tends to favor in its selection of texts for the exam. Common themes include:

- a heroic journey or quest
- self-determination or self-discovery
- coming of age or maturity (bildungsroman)
- awakenings or epiphanies: individual, spiritual, etc.
- disparity and oppression: class, economy, race, sex, etc.

In general, the AP Lit exam is going to present obscure texts in the multiple-choice section, presumably so that a greater percentage of students will be unfamiliar with them. Therefore, you cannot expect to study and know those passages and poems ahead of time. Instead, your success hinges on your careful reading and analysis of these passages and poems on test day.

No doubt you have already read some of the works listed in this chapter. To aid you in remembering the key concepts for those works, there is a graphic organizer presented at the end of this chapter called *Remembering Major Works*. This organizer is not meant to represent everything you might need to know about a certain text, but it gives you a concise format for recording a good summary of major novels or plays. It is meant to be a memory tool.

If you have read very few books at this point, use the *Key Concepts* section below to find books that you would enjoy reading and studying. Be sure to choose a variety, not all 18th-century British novels, for example. It is good to read old and new, American and British, fiction and drama. The key is to mix it up.

TEXTS OF LITERARY MERIT

The third free-response question on the AP Lit exam is open-ended. You are given a general prompt and are expected to apply that prompt to a literary work with which you are thoroughly familiar. I cannot impress upon you enough the importance of choosing a novel or a play of literary merit. If you do not, you risk a poor score.

You may believe that *Harry Potter and the Prisoner of Azkaban*, *Breaking Dawn*, or even *Green Eggs and Ham* is the most profound book you have ever read and you might even believe that it perfectly fits the prompt, but—and this is very important—if you choose such a book, you are taking a big risk. Not only will you have to defend your thesis, but you will also need to argue that the text you have chosen is of enduring literary quality. On the AP Lit exam you don't have time for such an argument!

Not only that, the College Board is also testing your ability to read and understand a complex text. While a great young adult novel might be engaging, it is probably not that complex. Choose your text wisely. You might want to save yourself time and possible grief by choosing five to seven novels or plays from the list that follows.

TITLES OFTEN CITED IN THE FREE-RESPONSE SECTION

The purpose of this list is to represent the various works that have been included or are representative of the titles cited on the AP English Literature and Composition Exam over the years. There would be no way for you to become familiar with all of these titles. But, this list reinforces the fact that it will be helpful to you to read a variety of literature from past and present authors representing diverse cultures.

A

The Aeneid

The Age of Innocence

Alias Grace

All the Light We Cannot See

Americanah

B

The Bell Jar

Beloved

Beowulf

The Bonesetter's Daughter

Breath, Eyes, Memory

Brighton Beach Memoirs

C

Ceremony

Cold Mountain

Crime and Punishment

D

Death in Venice

Death of a Salesman

Dracula

E

Exit West

F

Frankenstein

G

The Goldfinch

Great Expectations

Gulliver's Travels

H

Heart of Darkness

Home

Homegoing

The Hummingbird's Daughter

I

The Iliad

K

Kindred

King Lear

The Kite Runner

L

Lonely Londoners

M

Madame Bovary

Mama Day

The Mambo Kings Play Songs of Love

Man and Superman

Mansfield Park

The Metamorphosis

Midnight's Children

The Mill on the Floss
Mrs. Dalloway
My Ántonia

N

The Namesake
Native Son

P

Paradise Lost
A Passage to India
The Piano Lesson
The Picture of Dorian Gray
The Poisonwood Bible
The Portrait of a Lady
The Power of One
Pudd'nhead Wilson
Pygmalion

Q

Quicksand

R

A Raisin in the Sun
The Return of the Native

S

The Scarlet Letter
Song of Solomon
Sons and Other Flammable Objects
The Sound and the Fury

T

The Tempest

Their Eyes Were Watching God

Things Fall Apart

To the Lighthouse

W

Where the Dead Sit Talking

Wuthering Heights

BRIEF SUMMARIES OF FREQUENTLY CITED WORKS

The purpose of this chart is not to supplant your reading, but merely to give you a brief glimpse of these works so you may choose several to read. It is important to your success on the exam that you are familiar with several works of literary quality, such as those on this list. The "tags" below give you an idea of themes and key literary elements for the work. Remember that you should read widely, which means old and new works of British, American, and world literature.

For additional detailed summaries and descriptions like this one, you can consult a variety of internet study guides.

The Adventures of Huckleberry Finn by Mark Twain, published 1884	**Genre:** episodic/picaresque novel **Setting:** Mississippi River mid-1800s **Main characters:** Huckleberry Finn, Jim, Tom Sawyer, Miss Watson **Main Plot/Idea/Concept:** Huck, abused by his alcoholic father, escapes with a runaway slave named Jim. He struggles with whether or not to turn Jim in to the authorities. **Tags:** satire, American themes/setting, slavery, pragmatism vs. romanticism, dialect

Continued →

(Continued from previous page)

All the King's Men by Robert Penn Warren, published 1946 (won Pulitzer Prize in 1947)	**Genre:** novel **Setting:** 1930s, the American South **Main characters:** Willie Stark, Jack Burden, Anne Stanton, Adam Stanton **Main Plot/Idea/Concept:** Willie Stark turns from an idealistic lawyer into a charismatic and powerful governor. On his way, Stark embraces various forms of corruption and builds an enormous political machine based on patronage and intimidation. His approach to politics earns him many enemies in the state legislature, but his constituents are nonetheless drawn to his fervent populist manner. **Tags:** Huey Long, political corruption, nihilism, Calvinism, charismatic public figures
All the Pretty Horses by Cormac McCarthy, published 1992 (first book of *The Border Trilogy;* received National Book Award)	**Genre:** novel **Setting:** Texas, Mexico, 1949 **Main characters:** John Grady Cole, Lacey Rawlins, Jimmy Blevins, and Alejandra **Main Plot/Idea/Concept:** Sixteen-year-old John Grady Cole grew up on his grandfathers' ranch. After his grandfather's death, Cole learns the ranch is to be sold. He cannot face the idea of living in town, so he convinces his best friend to travel to Mexico, hoping they will find work as cowboys. **Tags:** coming of age, loss of innocence, the nature of evil

Anna Karenina by Leo Tolstoy, published 1873–1877 (serial publication)	**Genre:** novel **Setting:** 1870s, primarily Russia, including Moscow, St. Petersburg, and the provinces **Main characters:** Anna Karenina; Konstantin Levin, Vronsky **Main Plot/Idea/Concept:** Anna's battle pits her passion for Vronsky and yearning for independence against her marital duty, social convention, and maternal love. **Tags:** adultery, psychological novel, tragedy, self determination
Antigone by Sophocles, written c. 441 BCE	**Genre:** drama, tragedy **Setting:** ancient Greece, Thebes **Main characters:** Antigone, Creon, Ismene **Main Plot/Idea/Concept:** The major conflict is between Creon and Antigone. Creon has declared that the body of Polynices may not be given a proper burial because he led the forces that invaded Thebes. Nevertheless, Antigone wishes to give her brother a proper burial. **Tags:** individual vs. society, tragedy, feminism
As I Lay Dying by William Faulkner, published 1930	**Genre:** novel **Setting:** fictional Yoknapatawpha County, Mississippi, 1920s **Main characters:** Darl Bundren (Addie's son) and Anse Bundren (Addie's husband); 15 different characters tell the story in the first person **Main Plot/Idea/Concept:** The Bundren family sets out on a somewhat heroic journey to bury their mother. A series of setbacks and obstacles mar their journey. **Tags:** black humor, satire, flashback

Continued ➜

(Continued from previous page)

The Awakening by Kate Chopin, published 1899	**Genre:** novel **Setting:** 1899, Grand Isle, a popular summer vacation spot for wealthy Creoles from New Orleans. The second half of the novel is set in New Orleans, primarily in the French Quarter. **Main characters:** Edna Pontellier, Robert Lebrun, Adèle **Main Plot/Idea/Concept:** On vacation, Edna experiences a series of realizations and begins a quest for independence and self-fulfillment, but social conventions that limit her self-expression prove too much for her. **Tags:** feminism, self-determination, power of self-expression
Beloved by Toni Morrison, published 1987	**Genre:** novel (historical fiction) **Setting:** 1873, with flashbacks to the early 1850s, Cincinnati, Ohio, Kentucky, and Alfred, Georgia **Main characters:** Sethe, Denver, and Paul D., Beloved, Baby Suggs **Main Plot/Idea/Concept:** Sethe escapes from slavery, but kills her older daughter to keep her from being taken back to the South by her old master. A mysterious figure appears at Sethe's home, calling herself by the name on the dead daughter's tombstone. **Tags:** supernatural, oppressive effects of slavery

Billy Budd (Billy Budd, Sailor) by Herman Melville, written 1891, published 1924	**Genre:** novel **Setting:** 1797, four years into the Napoleonic Wars; an English warship, the *Bellipotent*, somewhere on the Mediterranean Sea **Main characters:** Billy Budd and Claggert **Main Plot/Idea/Concept:** Billy's natural innocence and goodness comes in conflict with evil, in the character of Claggert. **Tags:** Christian allegory, tale of the sea, individual vs. society, good vs. evil
Bless Me, Ultima by Rudolfo Anaya, published 1972	**Genre:** novel **Setting:** New Mexico in the 1940s, during and after World War II **Main characters:** Antonio (first-person narrator), Ultima **Main Plot/Idea/Concept:** This is the story of Antonio's growth from child to adolescent. Cultural traditions and his own family's expectations sometimes conflict with his own desire to be independent. **Tags:** Bildungsroman (coming-of-age story); magical realism
Candide by Voltaire, French, published 1759	**Genre:** novel, adventure, satire **Setting:** 1750s, various real and fictional locations in Europe and South America **Main characters:** Candide (whose adventures and experiences are related by a third person narrator) **Main Plot/Idea/Concept:** Candide and Pangloss's optimism is challenged by numerous disasters; Candide is expelled from his home for kissing Cunégonde; he wanders the world attempting to preserve his life and reunite with his beloved. **Tags:** Satire, irony, corrupting power of money, political oppression

Continued →

(Continued from previous page)

Catch-22 by Joseph Heller, published 1961	**Genre:** novel **Setting:** Pianosa, a small island off the coast of Italy, near the end of World War II **Main character:** John Yossarian, an Air Force captain and bombardier **Main Plot/Idea/Concept:** Yossarian struggles to stay alive, despite the many parties who seem to want him dead. **Tags:** satire, loss of religious faith, power of bureaucracy, symbolism
Ceremony by Leslie Marmon Silko, published 1977	**Genre:** novel, with poetry (Native American) **Setting:** primarily Laguna Reservation in the Southwest of the United States in the years following World War II; time is circular, events are remembered and foreshadowed **Main characters:** Tayo, whites, and Emo **Main Plot/Idea/Concept:** After recovering in a veterans' hospital, Tayo returns to his reservation. He must find a way to cure his mental wounds as well as to bring rain back to his people. **Tags:** non-linear structure, tradition, clash of cultures
The Color Purple by Alice Walker, published 1982	**Genre:** novel (epistolary) **Setting:** rural Georgia, 1910–1940 **Main characters:** Celie, Shug, Nettie **Main Plot/Idea/Concept:** Celie is verbally, physically, and sexually abused by several different men, lowering her self-esteem; she is a child woman with no voice, and no one to turn to. The story is told through a series of letters in Celie's voice. **Tags:** racism, sexism, self-discovery

Crime and Punishment by Fyodor Dostoevsky, 1866–1867	**Genre:** novel **Setting:** St. Petersburg, Russia, and a Siberian prison **Main characters:** Raskolnikov, Luzhin, Porfiry Petrovich, Svidrigailov, Raskolnikov's conscience **Main Plot/Idea/Concept:** Raskolnikov is a poor ex-student who conceives of and carries out his plan to kill an unscrupulous pawnbroker for her money. He will gain wealth and rid the world of a horrible person. Raskolnikov attempts to convince himself that murder is acceptable if it achieves a higher purpose. **Tags:** psychology of crime and punishment, poverty, alienation from society, religious redemption, moral dilemma
The Crucible by Arthur Miller, published 1953	**Genre:** play **Setting:** Salem, Massachusetts **Main characters:** John and Elizabeth Proctor, Thomas and Ann Putnam, Reverend Parris, Abigail Williams, and Reverend John Hale **Main Plot/Idea/Concept:** Abigail Williams leads a group of young girls who accuse local men and women of witchcraft partly to cover up their "sinful" nocturnal activities in the forest. John Proctor, who has committed adultery with Abigail Williams, tries to combat the hysteria. **Tags:** intolerance, greed, sin and forgiveness, tragedy, McCarthy Hearings (Red Scare) **Note:** Miller's play is based on real characters in the Salem Witch Trials

Continued ➡

(Continued from previous page)

Cry, The Beloved Country by Alan Paton, published 1948	**Genre:** novel **Setting:** 1940s, Ndotsheni and Johannesburg, South Africa **Main characters:** Stephen Kumalo, James Jarvis, Theophilus Msimangu, Absalom Kumalo, Arthur Jarvis **Main Plot/Idea/Concept:** Stephen Kumalo struggles against white oppression and the corrupting influences of city life that are destroying his family and his country. He travels to Johannesburg to search for his son who has been arrested for the murder of Arthur Jarvis. However, he is unable to save his son, who is sentenced to death. Afterward, Jarvis's father helps Kumalo to improve conditions in the village. **Tags:** Apartheid, fathers and sons, injustice, repentance
Death of a Salesman by Arthur Miller, published 1949	**Genre:** play **Setting:** 1940s, Brooklyn, Manhattan, and Boston **Main characters:** Willy Loman, Linda (his wife), Biff and Happy (his two sons) **Main Plot/Idea/Concept:** A washed-up salesman considers the value of his life and decides he can leave more to his family if he's dead and his life insurance policy provides for them. **Tags:** tragedy, The American Dream, flashback

A Doll's House by Henrik Ibsen, first published 1879	**Genre:** play **Setting:** Norway, late 1800s **Main characters:** Nora and Torvald Helmer, Kristine Lind, Dr. Rank, Nils Krogstad **Main Plot/Idea/Concept:** A young wife, who has forged her father's signature to gain funds to take her ill husband on a rest cure, finds herself about to be found out, a result that would bring shame upon her husband and threaten her marriage. **Tags:** women's rights, honor/duty, gender roles, marriage
An Enemy of the People by Henrik Ibsen, published 1882	**Genre:** play **Setting:** 19th-century coastal Norway **Main characters:** Dr. Thomas Stockmann, Peter Stockmann **Main Plot/Idea/Concept:** The town the Stockmanns live in has just invested a lot of money in new public baths, which they hope will pay off through an increase in tourism. The baths become popular and lucrative, but Dr. Stockmann discovers that waste from the local tannery is polluting the baths and making them toxic to users. Far from being rewarded for his community-minded act, Stockmann is ostracized for his unwillingness to go along with the cover-up. **Tags:** hypocrisy of political systems; disillusionment; illusion of truth

Continued →

(Continued from previous page)

Ethan Frome by Edith Wharton, published 1911	**Genre:** novel **Setting:** Massachusetts, late 19th and early 20th centuries **Main characters:** Ethan Frome, Zenobia (Zeena) Frome, Mattie Silver **Main Plot/Idea/Concept:** Ethan Frome is a married man who cannot act upon his feelings for another woman. **Tags:** social oppression, marriage
Frankenstein by Mary Shelley, published 1818	**Genre:** novel **Setting:** 18th-century Europe **Main characters:** Narrator: Robert Walton (in letters to his sister), Victor Frankenstein **Main Plot/Idea/Concept:** In college, Victor Frankenstein excels at the sciences and discovers the secret to giving life to the inanimate. He eventually creates his "monster." This classic novel explores the results of unchecked ambition. **Tags:** science fiction, horror, effects of ambition
The Glass Menagerie by Tennessee Williams, published 1945	**Genre:** play **Setting:** 1937, St. Louis **Main characters:** The Wingfield family: Tom, Laura, and their mother Amanda **Main Plot/Idea/Concept:** The family's situation is revealed through Tom's memories. Tom worries he will have to work at a meaningless job instead of writing poetry, which is more satisfying. Amanda is worried that Laura, who wears a brace on her leg and is overly shy, will never find a suitor. **Tags:** tragedy, family drama, symbolism, alienation

Great Expectations by Charles Dickens, serialized from December 1860 to August 1861	**Genre:** novel (coming of age) **Setting:** Kent and London, England, mid-19th century **Main characters:** Pip, Joe, Mrs. Joe, Estella, Miss Havisham, Magwitch **Main Plot/Idea/Concept:** A poor young boy finds himself the recipient of some money from an unknown benefactor and he seeks to improve his status in life. **Tags:** love, ambition, self-improvement, social class, symbolism, foreshadowing
The Great Gatsby by F. Scott Fitzgerald, published 1925	**Genre:** novel, novel of manners **Setting:** summer of 1922, New York City and Long Island, New York **Main characters:** Nick Carraway (narrator), Jay Gatsby, Daisy Buchanan **Main Plot/Idea/Concept:** Gatsby has accumulated a vast fortune so he may earn the affections of a woman of the "upper class," Daisy Buchanan, but his mysterious past stands in the way of his being accepted by her. **Tags:** 1920s, disparity among social classes, decline of the American Dream
Gulliver's Travels by Jonathan Swift, published 1726	**Genre:** satire (fictional narrative) **Setting:** early 18th century, primarily in Great Britain, but also in fictional lands such as Brobdingnag **Main characters:** Lemuel Gulliver, narrator **Main Plot/Idea/Concept:** Gulliver, a British surgeon, turns sea captain in four voyages that reveal to him the worst of human nature. **Tags:** satire, fantasy, adventure, politics

Continued ➝

(Continued from previous page)

Hamlet by William Shakespeare, written between 1599 and 1601	**Genre:** play **Setting:** medieval Denmark **Main characters:** Hamlet, Claudius, Polonius, Ophelia **Main Plot/Idea/Concept:** The ghost of the murdered king of Denmark asks his son Hamlet to avenge his death. **Tags:** foreshadowing, death and suicide, uncertainty of the future, treachery, moral corruption
Heart of Darkness by Joseph Conrad, 1899 (serialized), 1902	**Genre:** short novel, novella **Setting:** late 19th century, primarily the Belgian Congo **Main characters:** Marlowe, Kurtz **Main Plot/Idea/Concept:** A young sailor, Marlowe, joins a Belgian trading company and goes deep into Africa to meet a man named Kurtz. Kurtz, who had established himself with natives as a kind of god, had descended into madness. **Tags:** frame story, imperialism (arrogance of imperialism), madness, wastefulness, quest
Hedda Gabler by Henrik Ibsen, published 1890	**Genre:** play **Setting:** Norway, 19th century **Main characters:** Hedda Gabler, Jørgen Tesman, Miss Juliane Tesman, Mrs. Thea Elvsted **Main Plot/Idea/Concept:** Newly married Hedda does not love her husband and her new life with him bores her. Her husband's old rival reappears and threatens their economic security. **Tags:** feminism, self-determination, jealousy, suicide, dissatisfaction with marriage

Invisible Man by Ralph Ellison, published 1952	**Genre:** novel (modern) **Setting:** 1930s, American South, New York (Harlem) **Main character:** narrator is unnamed black man **Main Plot/Idea/Concept:** search for self vs. the oppression of racism **Tags:** blindness, racism, symbolism
Jane Eyre by Charlotte Brontë, published 1847	**Genre:** novel, (Gothic and romantic) English **Setting:** early 19th century, England **Main characters:** Jane Eyre, Mr. Rochester **Main Plot/Idea/Concept:** Jane Eyre, as an adult, tells the story of her young life so far, from an orphan to a love-torn woman. **Tags:** love, self-determination, social class, religion
Jude the Obscure by Thomas Hardy, first serialized, then published as a book in 1894	**Genre:** novel **Setting:** Southwest England **Main characters:** Jude Fawley, Arabella Donn, Sue Bridehead, Mr. Phillotson **Main Plot/Idea/Concept:** Jude Fawley is a stonemason who desires to be a scholar, and toward that end, teaches himself Greek and Latin. Before he can try to enter the university, he marries an unrefined local girl, Arabella Donn, but she deserts him within two years. He moves to Christminster and meets Sue Bridehead, his cousin, who becomes the love of his life. However, she marries Mr. Phillotson. Sue is unhappy in this marriage, partly because she loves Jude, so she leaves her husband and goes to live, unmarried, with Jude. Jude and Sue have several children together and are ostracized for their behavior. **Tags:** marriage, conventional morality, individualism

Continued →

(Continued from previous page)

The Jungle by Upton Sinclair, published 1906	**Genre:** novel (social criticism, muckraking) **Setting:** 1900, Packingtown, the meat packing section of Chicago **Main characters:** Jurgis Rudkus, Ona Lukoszaite, Teta Elzbieta Lukoszaite, Marija Berczynskas, and Phil Connor **Main Plot/Idea/Concept:** Jurgis Rudkus, a Lithuanian immigrant, and his extended family hope that by working hard they can share in the American Dream, but wage slavery and the oppression of capitalism turn their lives into tragedy. **Tags:** corruption, traditional values, symbolism, immigrant experience, evils of capitalism
King Lear by William Shakespeare, first folio 1623	**Genre:** play, tragedy **Setting:** England, 8th century BCE **Main characters:** King Lear of Britain; Lear's daughters Goneril, Regan, and Cordelia; Edmund, the bastard son of Gloucester **Main Plot/Idea/Concept:** King Lear decides to step down from his throne and divide his kingdom among his three daughters, but before doing so, he tests their loyalty. Goneril and Regan betray their father. **Tags:** madness, justice, authority versus chaos, betrayal, reconciliation, love and forgiveness, redemption, weather as a symbol

Light in August by William Faulkner, published 1932	**Genre:** novel **Setting:** 1920s in Jefferson, Mississippi and surrounding area **Main characters:** Joe Christmas, Gail Hightower, Lena Grove, Byron Bunch **Main Plot/Idea/Concept:** Joe Christmas is an adopted orphan who ends up killing his overly stern father. Years later, he is punished for his crime, but in the time intervening, he struggles for self-acceptance and to find his place in the world. **Tags:** flashback, alienation, burdens of the past, sense of self
Lord Jim by Joseph Conrad, published 1900	**Genre:** novel **Setting:** Indonesia **Main characters:** Jim (Lord Jim), Marlow **Main Plot/Idea/Concept:** A young British seaman named Jim becomes first mate on the *Patna*, a ship full of pilgrims traveling to Mecca. There is an accident and Jim, along with the captain and some others in the crew, abandons the ship and its passengers, a cowardly action for which he is eventually tried. It is at the trial that he meets Marlow, a sea captain who becomes Jim's friend and mentor. Marlow is the story's narrator. Jim's life toggles between his desire for redemption and his need to distance himself from the shame of his past. **Tags:** quest, human weakness, redemption

Continued ➡

(Continued from previous page)

Madame Bovary by Gustave Flaubert, serialized October 1, 1856, and December 15, 1856, tried for obscenity which made it notorious, published as a novel in 1857	**Genre:** novel **Setting:** 19th-century provincial France **Main characters:** Emma Bovary, Charles Bovary, Monsier and Madame Homais, Léon Dupuis, and Rodolphe Boulanger **Main Plot/Idea/Concept:** Emma Bovary is discontented with marriage, which leads her into a scandalous affair. Her spendthrift ways leave her husband in financial distress, but she finds she relies on his generosity and tries to help him. **Tags:** realism, Flaubert's greatest work
The Mayor of Casterbridge by Thomas Hardy, serialized first, then published 1886	**Genre:** novel **Setting:** fictional Casterbridge, mid-1800s **Main characters:** Michael Henchard, Donald Farfrae, Susan Henchard, Elizabeth-Jane Newson **Main Plot/Idea/Concept:** One night, drunk and angry with his wife, Henchard sells his wife and child to a sailor. After the sailor dies, Susan returns with her daughter and reunites with her former husband. **Tags:** honor, moral righteousness, reconciliation
Medea by Euripides, 431 BCE	**Genre:** play, Greek tragedy **Setting:** Corinth **Main characters:** Medea, Jason, King Creon (of Corinth), and Glauce, Creon's daughter **Main Plot/Idea/Concept:** Medea's husband Jason has turned her and her children away so he can marry King Creon's daughter, in hopes of advancing his social station. **Tags:** revenge, murder, tragedy

The Merchant of Venice by William Shakespeare, from 1596–98	**Genre:** play, comedy **Setting:** Venice **Main characters:** Antonio (a merchant), Shylock (a moneylender and a Jew), Bassanio, Lorenzo, Portia, Jessica and Nerissa **Main Plot/Idea/Concept:** Bassanio wishes to court the wealthy Portia, but he's squandered his fortune. He asks his friend Antonio to help him once again, but Antonio's fortune is tied up in his ships out to sea, so they engage the money lender, Shylock. The condition of the loan, if it is not repaid, is that Shylock may take a pound of flesh from Antonio. **Tags:** anti-Semitism, disguise, gender roles, marriage, Portia's famous speech on mercy
Moby Dick by Herman Melville, published 1851	**Genre:** novel **Setting:** 1830s or 1840s, aboard the whaling ship *The Pequod*, upon the Pacific, Atlantic, and Indian Oceans **Main characters:** Ishmael (narrator), Captain Ahab, Moby Dick (the white whale) **Main Plot/Idea/Concept:** Defying all odds, Captain Ahab commits his crew to hunting down and destroying Moby Dick because he sees him as representing all that is evil. **Tags:** epic adventure, allegory, quest, hubris

Continued →

(Continued from previous page)

Moll Flanders by Daniel Defoe, 1722	**Genre:** novel, episodic **Setting:** London, Virginia **Main characters:** Moll, her mother, numerous men, some of whom she marries **Main Plot/Idea/Concept:** The full title says it all: "The Fortunes and Misfortunes of the Famous Moll Flanders, Etc. Who was born in Newgate, and during a life of continu'd Variety for Threescore Years, besides her Childhood, was Twelve Year a Whore, five times a Wife (whereof once to her own brother), Twelve Year a Thief, Eight Year a Transported Felon in Virginia, at last grew Rich, liv'd Honest and died a Penitent. Written from her own Memorandums." **Tags:** alienation of lower classes, poverty, adventure, marriage, self-determination
Mrs. Dalloway by Virginia Woolf, published 1925	**Genre:** novel **Setting:** England, post–World War I **Main characters:** Clarissa Dalloway, Septimus Smith **Main Plot/Idea/Concept:** All of the present action takes place on one day in June. The author uses flashbacks to other times and locales. Mrs. Dalloway prepares for a party and thinks of her marriage and those she has loved. **Tags:** stream of consciousness, feminism, homosexuality, value of inner life (thoughts, emotions), effects of war

Murder in the Cathedral by T.S. Eliot, first performed in 1935	**Genre:** poetic drama **Setting:** Canterbury, England, 1170 (when Archbishop Thomas Becket was murdered) in the archbishop's hall and in the cathedral **Main characters:** Chorus, as in a Greek drama, comments on the action in the play. The archbishop, himself, knights, three tempters. **Main Plot/Idea/Concept:** Thomas Becket is murdered and martyred. **Tags:** individual versus authority, anti-fascism, power of church versus state
Native Son by Richard Wright, published 1940	**Genre:** novel (social protest) **Setting:** 1930s, Chicago **Main characters:** Bigger Thomas, Mary Dalton, Jan Erlone, Boris Max (narrated from Bigger's perspective) **Main Plot/Idea/Concept:** A young black man gets a job as a chauffeur for the Daltons, a wealthy white family. Bigger accidentally kills Mary and he flees, but is eventually caught and put on trial. **Tags:** oppression of racism, anti-Semitism, Communism, justice
Obasan by Joy Kogawa, published 1981	**Genre:** novel (historical) **Setting:** 1972 and World War II, Canada **Main characters:** Naomi Nakane, Obasan, Aunt Emily, Stephen **Main Plot/Idea/Concept:** Naomi struggles to reconcile herself with her painful past. **Tags:** Japanese Canadian relocation, World War II, clash of cultures

Continued →

(Continued from previous page)

Othello by William Shakespeare, published 1622	**Genre:** play, tragedy **Setting:** Venice **Main characters:** Othello, Desdemona, Iago, Roderigo **Main Plot/Idea/Concept:** Despite their differences in age, race, and experience, Othello and Desdemona marry and attempt to build a life together. The envious Iago attempts to sabotage their marriage by convincing Othello that Desdemona has been unfaithful. **Tags:** seeing and blindness, revenge, race
A Passage to India by E.M. Forster, published 1924	**Genre:** political novel **Setting:** Chandrapore, India, early 20th century **Main characters:** Dr. Aziz, Mrs. Moore, Miss Adela Quested, Ronny Heaslop **Main Plot/Idea/Concept:** Miss Quested accuses Dr. Aziz of attempting to sexually assault her in the nearby Marabar Caves. Aziz suspects Fielding of plotting against him with the English. **Tags:** colonialism
Portrait of the Artist as a Young Man by James Joyce, published 1916	**Genre:** novel, autobiographical novel **Setting:** 1882–1903, Dublin, Ireland **Main character:** Stephen Dedalus **Main Plot/Idea/Concept:** Stephen struggles with whether he should be loyal to his family, the church, and to Ireland, or to pursue his dream of being an artist. **Tags:** Irish independence, the church, self-determination

Portrait of a Lady by Henry James, serialized 1880–81, published as a book in 1881	**Genre:** novel **Setting:** Europe (England and Italy, primarily) **Main characters:** Isabel Archer, Gilbert Osmond, Pansy **Main Plot/Idea/Concept:** Isabel Archer inherits a fortune, but must fight to control her own destiny. **Tags:** old vs. new world, personal freedom, betrayal
Pride and Prejudice by Jane Austen, published 1813	**Genre:** novel **Setting:** Hertfordshire, England, turn of the century **Main characters:** Elizabeth Bennet, second eldest of a poor country gentleman, Mr. Darcy, George Wickam, and Jane Bennet **Main Plot/Idea/Concept:** The novel chronicles the experiences of the Bennet sisters and their love interests. **Tags:** social class, morality and moral judgment, manners, and marriage
A Raisin in the Sun by Lorraine Hansberry, published 1950	**Genre:** play **Setting:** Chicago **Main characters:** Walter and Beneatha Younger, their mother, and Walter's wife, Ruth **Main Plot/Idea/Concept:** A family has different views on how to spend an insurance settlement. They also fight against racial prejudice. **Tags:** dignity and honor, racism, gender roles, cultural assimilation

Continued ➡

(Continued from previous page)

Rosencrantz and Guildenstern Are Dead by Tom Stoppard, published 1967	**Genre:** play **Setting:** late 1500s, Hamlet's court **Main characters:** Rosencrantz and Guildenstern **Main Plot/Idea/Concept:** Rosencrantz and Guildenstern try to discover the cause of Hamlet's madness and, at the same time, their own purpose in the world. **Tags:** satire, black comedy, making choices
The Scarlet Letter by Nathaniel Hawthorne, published 1850	**Genre:** novel, romantic **Setting:** mid-17th century, Boston, Massachusetts **Main characters:** Hester Prynne, Arthur Dimmesdale, Roger Chillingworth **Main Plot/Idea/Concept:** A young woman whose husband is abroad, has an affair and gives birth to a child out of wedlock. She is publicly shunned by her Puritan society and forced to wear a scarlet letter "A" that stands for adulterer. The father of the child cannot bring himself to admit his role and must deal with his oppressive guilt. **Tags:** symbolism, morality, guilt, self-sacrifice
Song of Solomon by Toni Morrison, published 1977	**Genre:** novel **Setting:** 1931–1963, Michigan, Pennsylvania, and Virginia **Main characters:** Milkman Dead, Pilate Dead, Macon Jr. **Main Plot/Idea/Concept:** Milkman Dead tries to leave the confinement of his parents' home to become independent. However, restrictions of wealth and class, as well as ignorance of his family history, become impediments. **Tags:** adventure, magical realism, allusion (Biblical), racism

The Sound and the Fury by William Faulkner, published 1929	**Genre:** novel **Setting:** Easter weekend, 1928, and June 1929 (with flashbacks); Jefferson, Mississippi, and Cambridge, Massachusetts (Harvard University) **Main characters:** children of the Compson family: Benjy, Quentin, Jason, and Caddie, Quentin (Caddie's daughter), and housekeeper Dilsey **Main Plot/Idea/Concept:** A distinguished family falls from grace. **Tags:** nihilism, order and chaos, time, structure (four different narrators), stream of consciousness
A Streetcar Named Desire by Tennessee Williams, published 1947	**Genre:** play **Setting:** 1940s, New Orleans, Louisiana **Main characters:** Blanche DuBois, Stanley Kowalski **Main Plot/Idea/Concept:** Blanche DuBois, an aging Southern debutante, tries to flee a sordid past when she comes to live with her sister in New Orleans. She hopes to begin again and reclaim her "glory," but she is pitted against working class Stanley Kowalski, her sister's husband. **Tags:** tragedy

Continued →

(Continued from previous page)

Sula by Toni Morrison, published 1973	**Genre:** novel **Setting:** The Bottom, a predominantly black community in Ohio, from 1919–1965 **Main characters:** Shadrack, Eva Peace, Hannah Peace, Sula Peace, Nel Wright and Tar Baby **Main Plot/Idea/Concept:** Agriculturally worthless land given to blacks eventually becomes valuable to whites, who want to turn it into a golf course. However, the setting serves primarily as an anchor for the story of the Peace family and their friends and neighbors over the years. **Tags:** racism, poverty and hopelessness, good and evil, postwar stress
The Sun Also Rises by Ernest Hemingway, published 1926	**Genre:** novel **Setting:** Paris, France, and Pamplona and Madrid, Spain: 1924 **Main characters:** Jake Barnes, Brett Ashley **Main Plot/Idea/Concept:** Jake loves Lady Brett Ashley, but his impotence caused by a war wound hinders their relationship. Jake loses numerous friendships, and his life is repeatedly disrupted, because of his loyalty to Brett, who has a destructive series of love affairs with other men. **Tags:** Lost Generation, disillusionment

The Tempest by William Shakespeare, published circa 1611	**Genre:** play **Setting:** the Renaissance, on an island probably off the coast of Italy **Main characters:** Prospero, Miranda, Ariel, Calaban **Main Plot/Idea/Concept:** Prospero, the duke of Milan and a powerful magician, is banished from Italy and cast out to sea by his brother, Antonio, and Alonso, the king of Naples. Prospero seeks to use his magic to make these lords repent and restore him to his rightful place. **Tags:** the theater, magic, revenge
Tess of the D'Urbervilles by Thomas Hardy, published 1891	**Genre:** novel (Victorian) **Setting:** late 19th century **Main characters:** Tess Durbeyfield, Alec D'Urberville, Angel Clare **Main Plot/Idea/Concept:** Thinking they are "lost" aristocracy, the poor Derbyfields send Tess to state their case to the wealthy D'Urbervilles. There she is seduced by the unscrupulous Alec and becomes pregnant. After the baby dies, Tess tries to find her own way, eventually meeting and falling in love with Angel, but her past does not allow her to be happy. **Tags:** injustice, powerlessness, symbolism

Continued ➔

(Continued from previous page)

Their Eyes Were Watching God by Zora Neale Hurston, published 1937	**Genre:** novel (coming of age, spiritual journey) **Setting:** Florida, 1920s or '30s **Main characters:** Janie, Pheoby, Joe Starks, Tea Cake **Main Plot/Idea/Concept:** From poor plantation beginnings, Janie's quest to be her own person teaches her about love and life's joys and sorrows. **Tags:** dialect, self-determination, quest, race and racism, feminism
The Turn of the Screw by Henry James, published 1898	**Genre:** short novel, novella **Setting:** 1840s, Bly, a country home in Essex, England **Main characters:** Douglas, Flora, the governess, Mrs. Grose, Miss Jessel, Miles, Peter Quint **Main Plot/Idea/Concept:** The story is narrated by the governess, who fears the children in her care are being tormented by ghosts. **Tags:** psychological novel, ghost story, sexual repression, madness

Waiting for Godot by Samuel Beckett, first produced in 1953	**Genre:** two-act play **Setting:** a country road by a tree, 20th century **Main characters:** Estragon, Vladimir, Pozzo and Lucky **Main Plot/Idea/Concept:** Two men wait unsuccessfully for someone named Godot to arrive. They say he is an acquaintance but, in fact, hardly know him, admitting that they would not recognize him if they saw him. To occupy themselves, they eat, sleep, talk, argue, play games, and contemplate suicide—anything "to hold the terrible silence at bay." **Tags:** existentialism, life is a game
Who's Afraid of Virginia Woolf? by Edward Albee, first performed in 1962	**Genre:** play **Setting:** small New England university **Main characters:** George, Martha, Honey, and Nick **Main Plot/Idea/Concept:** George and Martha invite new professor Nick and his wife to their home after a party, where everyone had been drinking. George and Martha verbally abuse each other in front of their guests. In this play the illusion of 1950s perfection is exploded. **Tags:** marriage, social norms

Wide Sargasso Sea by Jean Rhys, published 1964–66	**Genre:** novel **Setting:** 1840s, Jamaica, the Windward Islands, England **Main characters:** Antoinette, Mr. Rochester, Christophine **Main Plot/Idea/Concept:** Rhys creates the unknown story of Bertha Mason, the insane wife of Edward Rochester in Charlotte Brontë's novel *Jane Eyre*. Mason, born Antoinette Cosway, is the daughter of former slave owners in Jamaica. **Tags:** colonialism and clashes of culture, slavery, race, religion, symbolism, written as prequel to *Jane Eyre*
Wuthering Heights by Emily Brontë, published 1847	**Genre:** novel (gothic) **Setting:** 1700s, Yorkshire England **Main characters:** Mr. Lockwood (narrator), Nellie, Heathcliff, Catherine **Main Plot/Idea/Concept:** Catherine is caught between her love for Heathcliff and her desire to be a gentlewoman, but she decides to marry the genteel Edgar Linton. **Tags:** social class, love, revenge

REMEMBERING MAJOR WORKS

Use this sheet to review a major work you have read that you might use for question three on the AP Lit exam.

Title:

Author:

Genre:

Literary Period, if significant:

Historical significance:

Setting: (time, place, and atmosphere, especially if the setting is a major element in the work)

Protagonist: (name, personality, appearance, etc.)

Antagonist(s):

Main conflict: (think in terms of what the protagonist wants/desires and what is keeping him/her from getting it).

Brief plot summary:

Resolution (of main conflict):

Major Themes: (What truths about life/human nature are revealed?)

Symbols:

Remarkable events/images/other elements:

Six Elements of Style:
Diction, Imagery, Tone, Syntax, Point of View, and Figurative Language

OVERVIEW

Every AP Lit exam will have questions about elements of style. It is important to know them for the multiple-choice section as well as for the essays. If you could study nothing else in preparation for the AP Lit exam, this would be the section to study.

It is far better, of course, to be familiar with all the concepts in this book because they function interdependently. The chapter that follows is a detailed look at basic literary elements. Notice the overlap between that chapter and this one. Instead of thinking of this overlap as repetitive, think of it as an indicator of how important these concepts are for you to know.

DICTION

Diction is often defined as the *author's choice of words*.

There are two ways to think of diction:

1) Specific *effect* of word choice: connotation and denotation

2) Overall style

CONNOTATION

In analyzing word choice, you should be looking at the connotation of a specific word choice and the effect of that association on the passage. Connotation is defined as the *emotional sense* of a word or the *cultural meaning* associated with a word. Connotations evoke associations. For example, the word "cancer" evokes fear, trepidation, and more.

In the passage from Cormac McCarthy's *The Crossing* (featured on an AP Lit exam), the author evokes a reverent tone, partly through his word choice. Words like "scrim," "celebrants," "sacred," "sects," and "penitent" have religious connotations. Careful readers will make these associations, which will help them connect with one of the main themes of the passage, which is that all living creatures, whether animal or human, are eternally connected through spirit.

In other words, noticing related words in a passage can provide clues to theme as well as become evidence for an answer in the multiple-choice section or for a claim you make in an essay.

Test Tip

Connotation: A Simple Strategy: When you read, if you begin to notice several words that fit together in connotative meaning, make a list of them in the margin (or circle them in the text). You are noticing a series of words that create a dominant impression. While this impression may not drive an essay thesis, it is probably a key to understanding themes or the author's purpose that is worth noting.

DENOTATION

Denotation refers to the *dictionary or precise meaning* of a word. Careful writers choose words carefully, often agonizing over the exact, right word that allows them to express an idea or an impression. Careful readers understand that word meanings have consequence in a sentence or a passage as a whole.

One of the main reasons students misread a poem or a passage is that they do not understand the vocabulary in the text. Unfortunately, you won't be able to consult a dictionary when you are taking the exam. Please see a list of potentially difficult vocabulary words in Chapter 9. While it is not plausible for you to know the definition of every word in every passage on the exam, if there is time, you should try to construe meaning from context for words that seem significant.

According to the College Board, questions asking you to determine the denotative meaning of a particular word from context will no longer be on the exam. However, you may still be asked to interpret words and phrases for their function. Understanding denotative and connotative meanings of words will always be important.

It is also important to be open-minded regarding the meanings of words. Be careful not to automatically attribute a common meaning to a word, especially when you are reading older texts, as meanings of words change over time. For example, the word "terrific" means "wonderful or great" in a contemporary context, but in the context in which it appears on a released exam, it means "terrifying." Another example is the word "awful," which means in its context "to be in awe of," but a careless reader might think it simply means "horrible."

To avoid misreading a text, especially when confronted with archaic language, try to determine word meanings from the broader context of the text.

Test Tip *Archaic, obscure, or overly specific language in poems or prose passages will generally be defined in footnotes.*

STYLE

Word choice also impacts overall style. You should think of style as the *voice of the writer*. Many decisions a writer makes—such as types and lengths of sentences (see syntax), words used (see diction), and the extent to which he or she uses imagery and figurative language—contribute to what is recognized as his or her style. For example, Hemingway's style is characterized, in part, by short, simple sentence structure, while William Faulkner is known for exceptionally long sentences.

Style can also mean something similar to tone.

Consider the difference in the styles of these two examples:

A) She was like, pizza is so, like, fattening. (Casual, conversational)

B) She understood that pizza was excessively high in fat and calories. (Formal)

You will be expected to implicitly understand that style impacts other elements in a passage, like characterization, attitude of speaker, and more. In the examples above, the speaker from example A could be characterized as less intelligent than the speaker from example B.

SOME TYPICAL STYLE DESCRIPTORS:

Authoritative: the voice is commanding and knowing

Emotive: the voice evokes emotion

Didactic: the voice is preachy, insistent

Objective: the voice is uncommitted, without judgment

Ornate: the voice is perhaps pretentious, flowery, or ostentatious

Plain: the voice is simple, straightforward, to the point

Scholarly: the voice is learned and authoritative, erudite

Scientific: the voice is precise and relies on the language of science (Latinate words)

You'll find a more comprehensive list of style descriptors at the end of this chapter.

IMAGERY

Imagery is not just one of the most important elements of poetry, it is also important to prose writers. Imagery is *language that engages the senses and evokes emotion*. As readers, we tend to relate to imagery on a gut level, responding with our emotions. The more detailed the imagery, the more we empathize or can put ourselves into the writing. Imagery is the collective impact of single images present in a passage.

TYPES OF IMAGERY

- Visual Imagery: what we can see
- Auditory: what we can hear

- Tactile: what we can touch
- Olfactory: what we can smell
- Gustatory: what we can taste
- Kinesthetic: sense of movement
- Organic: internal sense of being (feeling well or ill)

These sensory perceptions created through language are vicarious, meaning we experience them through the experience of the character or the narration. We might also consider these perceptions to be virtual. We don't actually experience them, but the emotions they evoke in us are real—the more vivid the imagery, the more real the emotion, or the more evocative the poem or passage.

To become good at recognizing good imagery, become good at looking for it and studying it. Stop when you recognize a particularly imagistic passage. Study it. What kind of imagery have you discovered? How do you feel as you experience the imagery? And most important, what is the effect of the imagery?

EFFECTS OF IMAGERY

- Helps establish tone
- Creates realistic settings
- Creates empathy in readers for characters
- Helps readers imagine themselves as part of a narrative

TONE

Tone is defined as *the attitude of the speaker toward another character, a place, an idea, or a thing.* In thinking of tone in this regard, it is important to pay attention not only to what a character or speaker does but also to what he or she says.

Sometimes we know more than the character does (dramatic irony) and this impacts our understanding of tone.

A passage or paragraph has a specific tone, or its emotional quality. This quality comes from details like imagery, diction (a character's speech, for example), and even syntax (short, simple sentences seem more serious or immediate and less reflective than longer, more ornate sentence types).

Tone is created in a variety of ways. Diction and imagery are major influences on tone. This is because images evoke emotions and certain words have emotional connotations. When you recognize tone, you most likely "feel" it first. But you also have to have an intellectual understanding of what you feel.

The first key to analyzing tone is to recognize it. You must acquaint yourself with typical tone descriptors (see the list at the end of this chapter), so that you aren't fumbling for a word to express what you think you see. The wider the variety of tone descriptors you use, the better you'll be at providing a precise analysis. In other words, if you characterize a passage as *melancholy* instead of *sad,* you are an AP English Literature student broadening your analysis.

In analyzing tone in a passage, it is also important to recognize shifts in tone. For example, if the passage begins in a light, carefree tone, then descends into despair, you will have recognized a vital reference point for analysis. Such shifts are not to be overlooked as coincidental or arbitrary. As you annotate passages, mark obvious shifts in tone (or style).

MOOD

Mood is related to tone. The term "mood" is most often used in association with setting, where the events take place. Think of mood as *the emotional quality of the setting.*

While there is most likely a prominent or dominant tone in a passage, be aware of tone shifts. If the tone changes suddenly, it can signal an epiphany or some change in a speaker or character's thinking. Tone shifts are critical markers in a passage.

See the end of this chapter for a comprehensive list of words to use when describing tone and mood.

SYNTAX

Syntax refers, in general, to *the order of words in a sentence.* Additionally, we use the term syntax to refer to sentence patterns, both specific types of sentences, patterns of sentences, or any other sentence variation that creates what could be called the "musicality" of the English language.

Such variation in sentences, through word order and pattern, creates interesting, fluent, readable prose.

Another way that syntax is worth noting as you read is that certain aspects of syntax, such as repetition and placement of ideas, are used for emphasis. So if an author wishes to reinforce key impressions or ideas, he or she can make use of a variety of syntactical patterns or techniques.

A study of syntax is important for several reasons:

- Sentences impact the narrative pace of a passage, making it read quickly or slowly, which therefore impacts the idea/theme.

- Certain types of sentences are better at emphasizing ideas, so key notions become prominent through placement, repetition, or parallel structure.

- There are sometimes questions in the multiple-choice section of the exam that ask you to identify types of sentences.

Syntax is often listed as one of the elements to analyze in a prose passage in the free-response section. However, it would be very rare for syntax to be the main analytical focus for any passage. Typically, elements like tone, diction, imagery, and figurative language are weightier indicators of an author's purpose or theme.

SENTENCE TYPES AND ATTRIBUTES OF SYNTAX

Sentence type or rhetorical examples	Attributes
Periodic	The most important idea comes at the end of the sentence.
Loose	The most important idea is revealed early and the sentence unfolds loosely after that.
Parallel	A parallel sentence (sometimes called a balanced sentence) contains parts of equal grammatical structure or rhetorical value in a variety of combinations. Some examples of parallel structures: 1. The dog ate voraciously, joyously, and noisily. (The verb *ate* is modified by three multisyllabic adverbs, which seems somewhat lofty in style for such a mundane act as a dog eating.) 2. Joyce was worn down by the constant invasion of her co-workers, by their insistent stares, by their noisy whispers, and by their unveiled disdain. She knew she had to find another job. (The parallel phrases are set off by commas; this is also an example of anaphora.)

Continued →

(Continued from previous page)

Sentence type or rhetorical examples	Attributes
Repetition Patterns	Types of repetition in sentences: **Anaphora:** the repetition of the same word or words at the beginning of a series of phrases, clauses, or sentences **Epistrophe:** the repetition of the same word or words at the end of successive phrases or clauses **Asyndeton:** conjunctions are omitted between words, phrases, or clauses **Chiasmus:** two corresponding pairs ordered this way: a/b/b/a **Polysyndeton:** the use of conjunctions between each word, phrase, or clause
Grammatical sentence types	1. Simple: 1 subject, 1 verb, modifiers, complements. Simple sentences are generally short and direct, and when used in combination with more complex sentences can add depth and texture to your writing. 2. Compound: 2 independent clauses joined by a comma and a coordinating conjunction (use the mnemonic "fanboys": _for, and, nor, but, or, yet, so_) to help you remember these conjunctions. 3. Complex: contains an independent clause and a (dependent) subordinate clause 4. Compound-complex: contains two independent clauses and a dependent (subordinate) clause

Sentence type or rhetorical examples	Attributes
Grammatical sentence purposes	1. Declarative sentence: makes a statement. 2. Imperative sentence: makes a command. 3. Interrogative sentence: asks a question. 4. Exclamatory sentence: makes an emphatic or emotion-filled statement.

MORE ASPECTS OF SYNTAX

1. Climax: the main idea or most important point in a sentence. The position of the climax may be varied for effect.

2. Cadence: the rhythm or "music" of a sentence that comes through parallel elements and repetition

3. Narrative pace: the pace or speed of a passage that comes through the following elements:
   - length of words
   - omission of words or punctuation
   - length of sentences
   - number of dependent/subordinate clauses
   - repetition of sounds

The shorter the words (fewer syllables) and the shorter and simpler the sentences, the faster the pace. Conversely, the longer the words (more syllables) and the longer, more complex the sentences, the slower the pace.

The 3 P's of Syntax

Prominence: Prominence refers to *the importance given an idea in a sentence.* Prominence is achieved both by placement and by repetition. Sometimes an idea is isolated in a short sentence where it is given sole prominence. If a word is ever set off alone as a fragment, it is being given prominence that best not be ignored. Instead, ask the question, "Why is this word isolated?"

Position: Position means *where the key idea is located.* It will most often come at the beginning of the sentence (loose sentence) or at the end of the sentence (periodic sentence). But sometimes, writers use nonstandard syntax, or inverted word order (especially in poems), to draw attention to certain words or ideas.

Pace: Pace is *the speed of the text* and generally complements the author's purpose. For example: Quentin's section in Faulkner's *The Sound and the Fury* is presented primarily in stream of consciousness, with fast-paced narration that emphasizes the character's frenetic and fragile state of mind. Another great example of how pace complements the writer's purpose is Maya Angelou's poem *Woman Work.* The first stanza, in which she describes all the tasks to be done, is meant to be read so fast that the reader actually feels tired after reading it. The rest of the poem is composed of four-line stanzas that read much, much more slowly. The images in these stanzas evoke peace, coolness, and rest.

Test Tip

Your own syntax is important in the essay section of the exam. See Chapter 15 for more on using sentence variety in your own writing.

POINT OF VIEW

Point of view is one of the most important elements of literature that you need to understand for the AP Lit exam. Most of the essay prompts imply an analysis of point of view, such as the speaker's response to an event, the speaker's attitude about an idea, etc. See Chapter 14 for a detailed analysis of prompts. Further, see Chapter 13 for more on point of view.

PRIMARY POINTS OF VIEW

First person: the narrator tells his/her own story using first-person pronouns (*I, me, we, us*). This point of view is limited by what the narrator can know, see, or understand. First-person narrators cannot always be trusted to assess a situation honestly. They may be blind to their own faults. Readers are expected to pick up on clues that reveal a first-person narrator's limitations.

Second person: the narrator uses second-person pronouns (*you*) to make immediate connections with readers (very rare point of view in fiction). You should never (only in exceptional cases) use second person in your own essays for the free-response section. As will be explained later, authoritative third person is best for essays.

Third-person limited: a third-person narrator tells the story from one character's point of view using third-person pronouns (*she, her, he, him, it, they, them*); this point of view is limited by the same constraints as first-person narrators.

Third-person omniscient: this third-person narrator is god-like, seeing and knowing all without constraints of time or space, seeing even beyond earthly existence. Third-person omniscient narrators sometimes digress into contemplative or philosophical forays.

Objective: an objective narrator tells a story like a video recorder would, simply revealing the sights and sounds it perceives (though not, of course, as strictly as that). You can recognize an objective narrator by that person's lack of emotion or personal interest in the subject.

FIGURATIVE LANGUAGE

The last element of style is figurative language, or *language not meant to be taken literally*. If we were to narrow down figurative language to one element, it would be metaphor. But, of course, the scope of what you are expected to know about figurative language and how it functions in a literary work goes beyond being able to recognize a metaphor. Being able to recognize various types of figurative language and being able to determine their effect is a key skill necessary for success on the AP Lit exam.

Authors and poets use figurative language to lead us to a deeper level of understanding and to see things in a new or even startling way. When confronted with complex metaphors, it is important to ask "what" and "why." What are we to see that we would not have seen without the metaphor, for example? Why is it there in the first place?

HOW TO RECOGNIZE FIGURATIVE LANGUAGE

- Learn the patterns of types of figurative language so that when you encounter them, you recognize them.

- Be open to finding figurative language: know that when a passage seems to be saying more than what appears on the surface, there is probably figurative language at work. Learn to read under the surface or, as is often said, "between the lines."

- Remember that poetry is almost a synonym for figurative language, meaning that there is a great deal of figurative language in poetry. Always be looking for it.

- Read carefully and don't settle for the most obvious interpretation.

- Look for examples of figurative language in your daily life: advertising, music lyrics, etc., in addition, of course, to the literature you're reading in preparation for the AP English Literature and Composition exam.

SPECIFIC TYPES OF FIGURATIVE LANGUAGE
(See also Chapters 6 and 7.)

Allegory: a type of symbolism. An allegory is *a description or a narrative (poetry or prose) with a secondary, or underlying, meaning.* An excellent example of allegory is George Orwell's *Animal Farm.* In that book, the situation, the characters, and the plot all have allegorical connections. (Briefly, the overthrow of a cruel farmer by the farm's animals is meant to parallel the Russian Revolution where the proletariat revolted against their dictator.)

Character allegory: In Dante's *Inferno*, characters often represent various ideal qualities. Vergil, the Roman poet (70 BCE–19 BCE), for example, stands for human reason. This allegorical meaning extends throughout the epic as Vergil serves as Dante's rational guide.

- Human virtues and vices were common character allegories in medieval literature, though they were generalized and not necessarily specific characters. For example, the seven deadly sins were often represented allegorically on stage or in literature. Gluttony, for example, was often portrayed as a corpulent slob.

Apostrophe (related to personification): *addressing something (or someone) non-living or incapable of response as if it could hear and respond,* such as "O, howling wind. . . ."

Irony: Irony exists when there is *a discrepancy between what is perceived and what is real.* There are four types of irony:

> **Verbal irony**—when what is said is different from what is meant

Dramatic irony—when the reader knows something a character does not know

Situational irony—when some aspect of the situation seems incongruous to either what seems appropriate or to what is expected

Socratic irony—when one feigns ignorance through questions or statements in order to expose truth or to extend an argument by exposing logical inconsistencies or factual errors

Test Tip

Being able to recognize irony and its effect is an excellent skill to cultivate. There are always several questions on the AP Lit exam regarding irony.

Metaphor: a *comparison of two dissimilar things in order to see one in a new way*

Metonymy (see also synecdoche): the *use of a closely related detail for the thing actually meant,* such as using "White House" to refer to the president or staffers, or "suit" (often as a pejorative) for a business executive

Overstatement (hyperbole): *saying more than the situation warrants.* The contrast illuminates the truth.

Paradox: a statement that consists of *two contradictory or incompatible elements;* paradoxical statements are startling and get us to think. They are a kind of metaphor that reveals the truth.

Personification: *attributing human qualities or characteristics to non-living or non-human things in order to create empathy*

Simile: essentially *a metaphor that uses "like" or "as"*

> **Epic or Homeric simile:** *an extended simile used in epic poems and Greek dramas.* A typical construction of an epic simile uses "just as" or "so then" to signal the comparison, though that is not *always* the case. The following example is from Homer's *Odyssey* (Fitzgerald translation):
>
>> *A man in a distant field, no hearthfires near,*
>> *will hide a fresh brand in his bed of embers*
>> *to keep a spark alive for the next day;*
>> *so in the leaves Odysseus hid himself,*
>> *while over him Athena showered sleep*
>> *that his distress should end, and soon, soon*
>> *in quiet sleep she sealed his cherished eyes.*

Synecdoche: *the use of a part for the whole,* such as "all hands on deck" or "the meeting can begin now that all the suits are here." Note: Synecdoche is sometimes identified as metonymy.

Symbol: *a thing, person, or idea that stands for something else.* Some symbols become iconic, that is, so well known that they're an accepted part of culture (e.g., water is a symbol of purity and or rebirth).

Understatement: *saying less than the situation warrants.* The contrast illuminates the truth.

Test Tip

Create an annotation symbol for metaphors, such as a star. Mark all metaphors as you read so they are easy to find and assess later.

STYLE DESCRIPTORS

The descriptors in the following lists come from questions about tone, style, attitude, and mood from released exams.

Tone

candid	laconic	sanctimonious	speculative
cynical	melancholy	sardonic	trite
detached	nostalgic	sinister	

Style

candid	detached	scornful	smug
cynical	sardonic	sinister	

Attitude

ambivalent	disdainful	indifferent	vindictive
anxious	eloquent	pretentious	whimsical
arrogant	fanciful	remorseful	
contemptuous	flippant	satirical	

Mood

apprehensive	quizzical	reproachful	solemn
elegiac	rapturous	satiric	suspenseful

MORE STYLE AND TONE WORDS

Style

accusatory	despairing	optimistic
acerbic	disdainful	patronizing
ambivalent	earnest	pessimistic
apathetic	gloomy	petulant
bitter	haughty	quizzical
callous	indignant	reflective
choleric	jovial	reverent
churlish	judgmental	ridiculing
conciliatory	malicious	sarcastic
condescending	mocking	sardonic
contemplative	morose	self-deprecating
contemptuous	objective	sincere
critical	obsequious	solemn
derisive		

Tone

caustic	forthright	poignant
colloquial	informal	ribald
didactic	intimate	satiric
effusive	lyrical	scholarly
erudite	matter-of-fact	terse
fanciful	objective	whimsical
formal	pedantic	

THINKING TOOLS

The following methods can help you generate and organize basic information you will need when analyzing a prose passage or poem. These easy-to-memorize acronyms should help you integrate the process of identifying basic literary and style elements into your general reading skills. In other words, if you use one or both of these thinking tools often, at some point, you will just think in this way, knowing to always look for these things.

Of course, identifying any basic element of literature is only a starting point. It's one thing to correctly identify the speaker or the audience. It's another to be able to go beyond the "what" of a work and extend your thinking to the "why" and "how." Analysis lies in determining the effect of literary elements in creating overall style and meaning.

SOAPSTONE

S	= Speaker
O	= Occasion
A	= Audience
P	= Point of View
S	= Subject
Tone	= Tone

SASS

S = Speaker
A = Audience
S = Situation/Occasion
S = Setting

THINKING TOOLS: DEFINITIONS

Speaker:

The speaker is the prominent voice in the work. This voice is always called the speaker in poetry, but may be referred to as a narrator or the narrative voice in prose. Do not confuse the author or the poet with the speaker, even though the two may overlap. Concentrate on only the voice within the work itself.

Occasion/Situation:

At times, the poet or author may set the work in a particular situation to give the message context. In Browning's *My Last Duchess*, the occasion is quite clear. The Duke is meeting with an emissary who represents the family of the next Duchess to arrange terms of the marriage. The occasion or situation in this poem is critical to understanding the Duke's monologue. Take care to use all available context clues to determine a logical occasion or situation. Sometimes the occasion is simply a time of year. Context for the message is what you ought to consider as you determine occasion or situation (essentially the same thing).

Audience:

The audience is the person or group to whom the speaker is speaking. Audience may or may not be directly expressed. In determining audience, you should think about who may benefit from the speaker's message. Many times, the audience is a general readership, but this is not always the case.

Point of View:

Point of view is related to the speaker in the most basic terms: first person, omniscient, etc. (See a more detailed explanation on different narrative points of view in this chapter.) But further, point of view also means the perspective or the position from which the speaker is an observer, so point of view can also be a contextual bridge to occasion or situation. A speaker witnessing first-hand the horrendous effects of mustard gas used on soldiers (as in Owen's poem, *Dulce et Decorum Est*) is a much more believable speaker than a purely third-person speaker.

Subject:

Most simply stated, the subject is the idea the poem is about. In the Sherwood Anderson passage you will read later in this book, the subject is a young man's journey away from home. In Shelley's poem, *Ozymandias*, the subject is the state of a once great memorial to a king that now lies nearly obliterated by time.

Tone:

Tone is the emotional quality of the work created through imagery and diction, or the speaker's attitude toward the subject or other element in the work. Attitude is, of course, how one feels about something.

Setting:

Related to occasion and situation is the setting. However, setting more specifically refers to the actual place and how it's described. Descriptive details in the setting often are strongly related to the work's tone.

PRACTICE YOUR UNDERSTANDING:

Seek out Wilfred Owen's poem *Dulce et Decorum Est* and use both of the thinking tools listed above in turn to identify various elements in the poem. Then, once having done that, write an essay using this prompt:

What is the effect of the last four lines of the poem, in which Owen includes a Latin phrase from the Roman poet Horace: "It is sweet and fitting to die for one's country."

Cite literary elements such as tone, imagery, style, and diction in your argument.

Fiction and Drama

On the AP Lit exam it won't be enough for you to simply identify literary elements. You will need to show your deep understanding of how such elements contribute to the meaning of the work. AP teachers speak of the need to go beyond the "what" to the "why" and "how."

In This Chapter

Overview

Elements of Fiction and Drama

Key Terms

Ten Common Novel Types

OVERVIEW

If doctors did not use precise medical terminology—"scalpel, stat" instead of "could you hand me that blade thing-y when you've got a moment?"—you would not want to be in surgery. It is important that doctors and nurses understand the language of their profession to do their jobs well. It is likewise important for you to understand the language we use to talk and write about literature.

ELEMENTS OF FICTION AND DRAMA

Following is a breakdown of key aspects of fiction and drama and how and why you should ponder each one. This section does not draw a distinction between long fiction (novel) and short fiction (short story or novella), as the following elements of literature apply to both.

The main distinction between fiction and drama is that in drama, the characters come to life and orally tell the audience the story. However, as in fiction, a play relies on character development, setting, plot, structure, and figurative elements.

On the left side of the chart is the concept (element of fiction) and one or two sample tasks. These tasks replicate the skills you may be asked to demonstrate on the AP exam. On the right side are definitions and detailed explanations related to each literary element. The "Take Note" section points out extra information that's good to know.

Understand that literary elements are not placed into a narrative as discrete pieces, but are complex components that often merge at critical narrative points. At an analytical level, literary elements become evidence of a writer's style and storytelling choices.

Sample Tasks	Concept Definitions and Details
Character	
Sample Tasks related to character: *Point out and explain how particular textual details reveal something about a character (motivations, choices, actions, etc.).* *Explain how a character's decisions, actions, choices, and speech reveal truths about him or her and explain the function in the larger work.* *Identify and explain what specific details reveal about a character, his or her perspective, values, motivation, or other aspect of belief or behavior.*	Types of characters: • Protagonist: the main character in the work • Antagonist: the character or force (even a non-human one) who opposes the protagonist • Foil character: a character whose characteristics or situation either mirrors (to some extent) the protagonist or contrasts with the protagonist, and, therefore, emphasizes traits in the protagonist • Dynamic character: a character who changes (develops or experiences personality growth) during the course of the work • Static character: those who remain unchanged or are unaffected by the events in a narrative. At times a protagonist can be static and as such presents an opportunity for readers to question how or why events did not impact the character as expected. • Archetypes: an archetype is a character or narrative pattern that is historically well-known (e.g., an exiled hero). The monomyth (or hero's journey) is an elaborate structure with defined stages. You will not be asked to identify particular archetypes on the exam.

Continued →

(Continued from previous page)

Sample Tasks	Concept Definitions and Details
	Ideas about characters: • Agency and Motivation: Agency refers to a character's ability to steer or control one's actions. Motivation is the reason the character chooses a course of action. • Characters generally change over the course of a narrative. Changes can range from external (everyone realizes it) to internal (only the character knows it). • Epiphany: an epiphany is a sudden realization or insight. It's that "lightbulb" moment when one says, "Oh, now I get it."
Take Note ➝	Through presentation of characters in a fictional work, an author can explore a wide range of topics and themes (see Chapter 12), which allows readers to experience diverse values, beliefs, global situations, and cultural norms. Pay attention to the aspects of a narrative that indicate what motivates a character's thoughts, actions, and decisions. Always be asking "why." The choices characters make reveal what they value. Sometimes what characters say or do contrasts with how they feel or what they believe, and such contrasts often reveal truths.

Sample Tasks	Concept Definitions and Details
Setting	
Sample Task related to setting: *Identify and explain how the setting conveys social values in a literary work.*	What is a setting? • Time, place, and historical context (beliefs, values) of a narrative. Impact of setting: • Setting helps to establish the mood and atmosphere of a narrative. Both mood and atmosphere are related to tone and the emotional quality of the story. • A setting can sometimes serve as a character in a narrative, particularly when the setting contains antagonistic elements against which characters are pitted. Setting in a play or drama: • The setting of a play is often obvious in set design, but not exclusively. • Characters can reveal truths about setting. The title of Ibsen's play is *A Doll's House*. Think of how Nora's interaction with her children and her husband help establish setting in ways a physical set design could not. • In the play *Our Town*, by Thornton Wilder, the sets are minimal on purpose. Addition details of the setting are given through narration and characters.
Take Note ➡	A powerful setting is drawn in Zora Neale Hurston's novel *Their Eyes Were Watching God*. Not only does the main character fight cultural stereotypes, she also must battle nature.

Continued ➡

(Continued from previous page)

Sample Tasks	Concept Definitions and Details
Plot/Structure	
Sample Tasks related to plot or structure: *Explain how contrasts function in a literary work.* *Explain how a particular sequence of events functions in a literary work.*	What is plot? <ul><li>A plot is the series of events in a work of literature. These events often have a cause/effect relationship. A well-structured plot builds to a climax and is resolved at the end of the work.<ul><li>The resolution of the central conflict can produce catharsis or emotional release. The level to which a reader experiences catharsis is tied to how closely he or she is able to identify with or empathize with the characters and situation.</li><li>Most plots "tie up" nicely, but some leave readers wondering what will become of characters in the future. Such endings are called unresolved endings. Such endings are open to diverse interpretations.</li></ul></li><li>Within the plot, characters are placed in conflict (a character vs. an internal or external force) against which they either triumph or fail.</li><li>Types of conflicts are listed below:<ul><li>Person vs. another person</li><li>Person vs. a group or social entity</li><li>Person vs. a non-human entity, such as nature, technology, etc.</li><li>Person vs. an inner conflict or dilemma, such as competing values or other psychological tension.</li></ul></li></ul>

Sample Tasks	Concept Definitions and Details
	• Plot events can be arranged (see structure) in a variety of ways. The list below is not inclusive of all methods.
	▸ Plots are typically ordered chronologically, by time in the order events occur.
	▸ Chronological order can be interrupted by flashbacks, a device the narrator uses to relate scenes from the past.
	▸ Foreshadowing refers to the times an author hints at something that lies in the future of the narrative.
	▸ *In media res*: Latin for "into the middle of things." Authors sometimes choose to begin in the middle of a conflict, rather than at the beginning.
	▸ Some narratives are arranged in sections by character: each one told from a different character's perspective.
	Importance of structure
	• Structure refers to the way an author arranges various parts and sections in a work to tell a story. The sequence and arrangement of these parts impact a reader's interpretation.

Continued ➔

(Continued from previous page)

Sample Tasks	Concept Definitions and Details
	Other plot/structure elements: • Stream of consciousness is a narrative style in which a character's thoughts, feelings, and reactions are presented in a continuous flow of language uninterrupted by narrative description or dialogue. • Suspense is created when an author omits information readers want to know or fails to answer questions. • Tension, related to suspense, is less about what you don't know and more about your anxiety related to characters or events. A high level of concern is tension. A feeling of fear because you don't know what will happen next is suspense.
Take Note ➞	It is not enough to relate only what happens (you'll end up with a plot summary). You must show how an event functions in the work as a whole. Be open to and aware of atypical arrangements of plot, which can lead to insightful reading of a narrative. Consider variants in plot and structure and how they impact narrative tension, suspense, and theme development.

Sample Tasks	Concept Definitions and Details
Point of View/Narration	
Sample Task related to plot or structure: *Explain the effect of a narrator's reliability on a literary work.* *Point out and explain literary details that reveal a narrator's perspective.* *Discuss the impact of alternative or contrasting points of view.*	General points of view: • First-person point of view: narration using first-person pronouns in the voice of the protagonist (or sometimes another character). This narrator can only comment on events that he or she can witness. • Third-person omniscient: narration using third-person pronouns. "Omniscient" means "all-knowing." An omniscient narrator is an outside observer, but is quite agile and can move from time and place easily and can function beyond physical limitations. • Third-person limited: the author narrates the story from the close perspective of one character (not the protagonist) which creates the personal immediacy and intimacy of a first-person narrative, but allows for a different perspective, often commentary on the protagonist. Types of narration/narrators: • Reliable narrator/unreliable narrator: when you detect bias in a narrator's perspective, you may construe the narrator is unreliable. Also, first-person narrators who say one thing and do another are usually unreliable. • Intrusive narrator: one who directly addresses the reader.

Continued ➜

(Continued from previous page)

Sample Tasks	Concept Definitions and Details
	Other important aspects of narration: • Narrative distance: refers to the physical, chronological, personal, or emotional connection or investment of the narrator to the events or characters in a narrative. Narrative distance can intensify tension by creating added anxiety in the reader. Sometimes authors insert their personal beliefs or biases into their work, through narrative passages or dialogue. However, it would be an incorrect assumption to construe that the narrative stance in any work is autobiographical or a direct express of an author's beliefs.
Take Note ➜	An omniscient narrator may know all but not necessarily tell all. Suspense and tension are created when questions go unanswered or details are purposefully omitted. A character's perspective (way of looking at things) is based on his or her personality, environment, culture, relationships, experiences, etc. Perspective is not the same as point of view. Perspective is how a character sees his or her situation, while point of view is the literary position from which the events of the story are told.

Sample Tasks	Concept Definitions and Details
Figurative Language	
Sample Tasks related to figurative language: *Identify and explain the function of figurative language in a character's course of action.* *Identify and explain the function of figurative language in the development of suspense in a narrative.*	Literal vs. figurative: The literal term in a comparison exists in temporal reality or is present in the mind. An author sees a tulip but thinks of a Venus flytrap. The tulip is present; but the Venus flytrap is imagined. The imagined thing is the figurative term. Direct metaphor: This metaphor compares a literal term to a figurative term using "is." Implied metaphor: The comparison is made without mentioning the literal term. Only the figurative term is used. Extended metaphor: The comparison is drawn out, often by use of examples, over the passage or chapter. Extended metaphors are common in poetry. Simile: Comparing a literal term to a figurative term using "like" or "as." Conceit: an elaborate, often scientific, comparison (metaphor). Symbol: a person, place, or idea that stands for or represents something else. Some symbols change over time and rely on cultural context for meaning. Some symbols have remained standard through history and through common use have become iconic; they are considered archetypes. You will not be expected to name or identify archetypal symbols.
Take Note ➞	All figurative language is a writer comparing something to something else to express a new way of thinking about the original idea or thing. Insight is a deep understanding that often arises when one says, "Hey, this is just like that."

KEY TERMS

It is critical to know these terms well. The starred terms (★) are those that have appeared more prominently on released AP Lit exams.

1. **allegory**: a narrative or description with a secondary or symbolic meaning underlying the literal meaning. *Life of Pi* is a novel of survival in which the lifeboat voyage represents a spiritual journey.

2. ★ **allusion**: a reference to something in previous literature, history, or culture that adds to or emphasizes a theme of the work.

3. **anecdote**: a clever little story; a short account of an interesting situation.

4. **antihero**: a protagonist whose attributes are opposite of what is expected of heroes. Antiheroes may be confused, powerless, victimized, or simply pathetic. Huckleberry Finn is an antihero.

5. **archetype**: a symbol that recurs often enough in literature over time to be easily recognizable, such as water as a purifying element or the sun as knowledge; also includes character types that are common: prodigal son, wise grandfather, etc.

6. ★ **atmosphere**: the emotional quality of the setting. See also "mood."

7. **epiphany**: a moment of insight, spiritual or personal; a character's sudden revelation about life or his or her own circumstances.

8. **eulogy**: a speech given at the memorial or funeral service in remembrance of one who has died.

9. ★ **extended metaphor**: a detailed or complex metaphor that is evident throughout a work.

10. **foil**: a character who possesses traits that emphasize the characteristics and qualities of another character, generally the protagonist, either by being similar to or opposite from that character.

11. ★ **imagery**: language that appeals to the senses. Images are emotionally evocative. There are seven types of imagery: visual (sight), auditory (sound), tactile (touch), olfactory (smell), gustatory (taste), kinesthetic (movement), and organic (internal sense of being).

12. **invocation**: a prayer or a statement that calls for help from a god or goddess. *The Odyssey* begins with Homer's invocation: "Sing in me, muse, and through me tell the story. . ."

13. ★ **irony**: a discrepancy between appearance and reality. There are three types of irony: verbal (when what a character says is different from what he means); dramatic (when the reader knows something a character does not know); and situational (when something in the situation is incongruous with what may be expected).

14. ★ **metaphor**: a metaphor compares two generally dissimilar things (objects, places, ideas, etc.) in order to show something new or to help readers see something in a new way.

15. ★ **mood**: the dominant tone in a piece of literature; typically the emotional quality of the scene or setting.

16. **motif**: a recurring element, an image or idea, in a work of literature, whose repetition emphasizes some aspect of the work (theme, plot, etc.).

17. **parable**: a short tale that teaches through example. Parables usually teach a moral or even religious lesson; they teach people about how they ought to live.

18. **paradox:** a situation or statement containing contradictory elements which nonetheless seem plausible or true.

19. **parody:** a work of satire where the author imitates the language and form of another work to ridicule the author or work.

20. **soliloquy:** primarily found in Shakespeare's plays, a soliloquy is a monologue, one character on stage, or in the spotlight, who relates his/her plight. Hamlet's famous "To be or not to be" soliloquy is an example. Soliloquies are not meant to be heard by other characters.

21. **symbol:** a person, place, thing, or idea that represents something else.

22. **syntax:** in general, the order of words in a sentence that results in various sentence types used for a variety of rhetorical effects (see Chapter 5).

23. ★ **tone:** the speaker or narrator's attitude towards something or the emotional quality of a passage (see Chapter 5).

24. **verisimilitude:** the quality in literature of being true to life; details seem realistic and believable, even if the setting is supernatural.

25. **vernacular:** the ordinary, everyday speech of a region.

Test Tip

It is difficult to understand literary elements out of context. As you read, identify various elements and make margin notes about their significance in the passage. See Chapter 10 on "Engaged and Active Reading."

TEN COMMON NOVEL TYPES

Note: Many books can be classified in more than one way.

1. **Bildungsroman (novel of education) or coming-of-age novel**: the protagonist is a child whose experiences teach him or her about the realities of the adult world. This transformation is often complex, painful, and filled with disillusionment.

2. **Dystopian novel**: presents readers with an apparent perfect (Utopian) society where human life is somehow diminished. Dark, prophetic themes: oppression, abuse of power, loss of individuality.

3. **Epistolary novel**: consists of letters written by one or more characters.

4. **Gothic novel**: characterized by dark, mysterious setting; has supernatural elements, especially ghosts. Gothic novels tend to be highly emotional, even melodramatic.

5. **Historical novel**: story is immersed in historical events; characters interact with history.

6. **Novella**: prose fiction longer than a short story, but shorter than a novel.

7. **Novel of manners**: the author details the social customs of an era and/or the social behaviors of a particular social group.

8. **Picaresque novel**: an episodic novel (string of episodes or adventures) starring a picaro or rogue (a person of low social status) who wanders or has adventures.

9. **Social novel**: concerned with the effect of societal institutions and social conditions on humanity.

10. **Utopian novel**: presents an ideal (perfect) society free from typical social problems.

Poetry

OVERVIEW

It is standard for two poems to be included in the multiple-choice section of the AP Lit exam. There will also be one poem to analyze in the free-response section. Therefore, it is important to have a good background in poetry. Just as it is important to stretch your intellect by reading a wide variety of novels and plays, you should also push your limits by reading challenging poems. At the end of this chapter I have listed twenty "must read" poems. By listing these poems, I am not suggesting that they are the only poems you should read, but they are poems that are often anthologized, often studied in AP Lit courses, and they will provide you with a good beginning for your study of poetry.

One of the most difficult things for students to conceive of as they read poetry is how figurative language functions in a poem. Poems are, by their nature, full of figurative language: metaphor, simile, personification, and more. Reading beneath the surface is critical to understanding a poem. (See Chapter 10, "Engaged and Active Reading" for more help with reading a text closely.) Poetry begs to be read several times, and in your preparation for the AP Lit exam, you need to train yourself to diligently and carefully read complicated poems as well as prose pieces.

This chapter will acquaint you with the poetry terms and concepts you are most likely to encounter on the AP Lit exam. Add unfamiliar terms in this chapter to your deck of flash cards. Further, look for evidence of poetic terms and devices in your daily life, particularly in song lyrics. Poetry is more common than you think.

ELEMENTS OF POETRY

Following is a summary of key aspects of poetry related to the AP English Lit exam, particularly as they relate to skills and tasks.

On the left are the concept (element of poetry) and at least two sample tasks. These tasks replicate the skills you may be asked to demonstrate on the AP exam. On the right are the definitions and detailed explanations related to each literary element. The "Take Note" section points out extra information that's good to know.

Remember that poetry and fiction often overlap. Poetry may contain elements of fiction, such as character, setting, and theme. So, what you learned in the previous chapter can apply here, particularly the section on figurative language. Poetry, of course, does differ from fiction, so this chapter details unique elements of poetry that you need to know.

Keep in mind that it is never enough to point out, for example, an allusion in the second stanza of a poem. Your response should also include the effect of that allusion on the work as a whole.

Sample Tasks	Concept Definitions and Details
Structure	
Sample tasks related to structure: *Explain the function of structure in a poem.* *Explain the function of contrasting elements within a poem.*	Forms of poetry • Open form (free verse): Open-form poems are free from specific rules of structure, but still differ from prose in that they may contain short lines, make use of stanzas, and contain other elements of poetry. • Closed form (or fixed form): Closed-form means that rules regarding number of lines, syllables per line, a metrical pattern, a rhyme scheme, or other construct is dictated by the form. There are numerous forms in poetry. One simple example is haiku, a three-line poem with a syllable requirement per line (5, 7, 5). • Continuous form: There are no stanza breaks. • Stanzaic form: The poem includes at least one stanza break. Watch for shifts in rhetorical purpose when moving from one stanza to another. Logical relationships are often revealed by stanza breaks. • Line breaks: Unlike prose, where a line wraps based on the page margins, a poet makes conscious decisions about when and where to break a line. A line of poetry does not necessarily constitute a grammatically complete "sentence," and thought units (clauses, phrases) often continue from one line to the next. Think about the effect of line breaks in an open form poem.

Continued ➡

(Continued from previous page)

Sample Tasks	Concept Definitions and Details
	Poetic patterns (find more on this later in this chapter) • Meter: the repetition of stressed and unstressed syllables that creates a musicality to poetic language. • Rhyme scheme: a designated repetition of rhymes. • Closed-form patterns dictate anything from number of stanzas, lines per stanza, rhyme schemes, metrical pattern, etc. Contrasts • Pay attention to general shifts in tone, point of view, character, narration, perspective of the speaker, setting, and imagery. • Stanza breaks often reveal contrasting elements. • Elements may be juxtaposed for rhetorical effect. Setting context • Epigraph: a short reference, quotation, or note set at the opening of poem to provide context. • Do not skim over epigraphs. Consider them as part of the poem's meaning. Poems in AP Lit exams are often accompanied by extra help to students with introductory statements, definitions of archaic words, or more. But such information is not to be used as evidence for interpretation.

Sample Tasks	Concept Definitions and Details
Take Note ➞	You will not be expected to point out particular forms or specific metrical patterns in poetry on the exam.
	Pay attention to stanza breaks. Poets don't generally break a poem arbitrarily. There is a reason, and likely stanza breaks contribute to the poem's meaning.
	Line breaks are often used for emphasis, especially in open-form poems.
	Because poems are, by their nature, short, all parts of a poem "matter." Pay close attention to parallels and contrasts for clues to meaning.
	Placement also matters in a poem. Study the ideas revealed in a poem's stanzas and determine their relationship.
Setting	
Sample tasks related to setting: *Identify and explain how the setting conveys social values in a literary work.* *Identify and explain how elements of poetry establish setting.*	What is a setting? • Time, place, and historical context (beliefs, values) of a poetic narrative. Impact of setting: • Setting helps to establish the mood and atmosphere of a narrative. Both mood and atmosphere are related to tone and the emotional quality of the story. • A setting can sometimes serve as a character in a poem, particularly when the setting contains antagonistic elements against which characters are pitted. Setting is integral to the poetic context in a text. Use time, place, culture, and history as clues to overall meaning.

Continued ➞

(Continued from previous page)

Sample Tasks	Concept Definitions and Details
Take Note ➞	The setting of a poem is established in various ways: sometimes direct exposition is used, but generally a setting is revealed through images, allusions, and figurative language.
Point of View/Narration	

Sample tasks related to point of view/narration:
 	
Point out and explain the function of literary details that reveal a speaker's perspective.
 	
Discuss the function of alternative or contrasting points of view.
	Poetic Point of View
	• We refer to the voice in a poem as the speaker. The speaker may assume the following points of view:
	  ▸ First person
	  ▸ Third person
	  ▸ Objective
	• The speaker is to be considered separately from the poet. While some poems are autobiographical, the intimate nature of a poem often leads students to assume every poem is about the author. Always consider the speaker of a poem as a separate identity from the poet.

Take Note ➞	A speaker's perspective or way of looking at things can be inferred from details given in a poem. Always consider the contextual information in the poem as a whole when determining a speaker's perspective.

Sample Tasks	Concept Definitions and Details
Imagery	
Sample task related to imagery: *Identify and explain the function of a single image or prominent imagery in a poem.*	Find more about imagery later in this chapter. • A collection of images is called imagery. • Imagery is one of the main qualities of poetry. • Strong images create immediacy by placing the reader in the setting and context of the poem. • Strong images evoke emotive responses in readers. • Analyze images based on their effect. • An image can be literal or figurative but is never used without purpose.
Take Note ⟶	Link imagery with language to determine a poet's purpose. Determine the value of individual poetic elements as they relate to the impact on the whole poem.

Continued ⟶

(Continued from previous page)

Sample Tasks	Concept Definitions and Details
Figurative Language	
Sample task related to figurative language: *Identify and explain the function of a metaphor or simile or other prominent figurative language.*	Literal vs. figurative: The **literal term** in a comparison is the thing that exists in temporal reality or the material world. The **figurative term**, while it may be a real, material thing, is likely not "there" in the moment the poet conceives of the comparison. Therefore, it is safe to say the figurative term exists in imagination. For example, a poet may see a daffodil and think of fresh-churned butter. The daffodil is present; the butter is imagined. The imagined thing is always the figurative term. • Direct metaphor: Comparing a literal term to a figurative term using "is." • Implied metaphor: The comparison is made without mentioning the literal term. Only the figurative term is used. • Extended metaphor: The comparison is drawn out, often by use of examples, over the passage or chapter. Extended metaphors are common in poetry. • Simile: Comparing a literal term to a figurative term using "like" or "as." • Conceit: an elaborate, often scientific, comparison (metaphor). Conceits, the preferred metaphoric construct of the metaphysical poets like John Donne, often make complex associations between nature and an individual.

Sample Tasks	Concept Definitions and Details
	• Hyperbole: an exaggeration that draws attention through contrast.
	• Understatement: stating or showing less strongly than the facts merit.
	• Personification: giving a human trait to a non-human being or object in order to characterize.
	• Allusion: a reference to history, culture, or literature that deepens meaning based on shared understanding. Allusions are only useful if a reader is able to grasp them.
	• Paradox: contrasting elements juxtaposed in an image or metaphor that reveals something true.
	• Irony: see Ch. 5 for details regarding irony.
	• Symbol: a person, place, or idea that stands for or represents something else. Some symbols change over time and rely on cultural context for meaning. Some symbols have remained standard throughout history and through common use have become iconic; they are considered archetypes. You will not be expected to name or identify archetypal symbols.
Take Note ➝	Being "in the know" regarding allusions is a matter of being well read. When a poet refers to "Poseidon," your familiarity with the Percy Jackson series of books may help you understand the allusion. With most allusions, you either get it or you don't. When you do, allusions deepen your understanding of the poem.

Continued ➝

(Continued from previous page)

Sample Tasks	Concept Definitions and Details
Language/Diction	
Sample task related to language/diction: *Explain the function of word choice, imagery, and symbols.*	• Connotation: the social, cultural, or emotional association of a word. • Tone: the general emotional quality of a word or phrase or the revelation through diction of the speaker's attitude toward a subject. • Word choice: a poet's decision to use one word over another for a precise purpose. • Alliteration: the repetition of beginning sounds in words in close proximity. • Ambiguity: textual uncertainty that allows for various interpretations of a text. Due to the figurative nature of poetry, poetic language is often ambiguous. Antecedents and referents: Often, determining what's what in a poem requires close analysis of clauses and phrases, particularly when they're ambiguous. An "antecedent" is a word, phrase, or clause that comes before its "referent," which is generally a pronoun but can also be a noun, a phrase, or a clause. Use logic (what makes sense) and grammatical proximity (the closest antecedent is typically the correct one, though not always) as tools to solve these puzzles.
Take Note ➡	Unlike a novel, every word in a poem "counts." Skipping over several words because they are unfamiliar can lead to a misreading of a poem. Instead, infer word meanings from context clues. On past exams, there were several questions requiring close analysis of antecedents and referents.

WHAT IS A POEM MADE OF?

IMAGERY

Imagery is what occurs when poets use words that appeal to our senses: we perceive, through his or her words, an idea or image. These images can appeal to all senses: sight, hearing, touch, smell, and taste.

Imagery is important in a poem because it is language that allows us to be transported to another place, time, and experience, which, if the image is effective, allows us to understand the emotion being conveyed in the poem. Imagery is also one of the main tools poets use to create a specific tone.

We can only know the world through our senses. We perceive first and reason second. Imagery is critical to understanding. Imagery allows the poet to show us meaning by taking us into the environment of the poem.

"Imagism" refers to the idea that an image, presented on its own, in a poem, has the power to unite the poet and the reader/listener in the exact impulse or experience that led the poet to write the poem in the first place.

DICTION

Diction is primarily defined as the poet's choice of words. Since poetry, of all literary forms, uses the least number of words to accomplish its task, each word is important and must be chosen for its exactness. Poets work to eliminate unnecessary words that would otherwise obscure the essential language of a poem. Therefore, glossing over words instead of reckoning with them as you read is likely to result in misunderstanding on your part.

How does a poet choose the exact word? Three reasons make sense:

Sound: How does the word sound? Does the sound contribute to the meaning, to the overall sound scheme, or does it interrupt or interfere? See the section on sound below for specific aspects of sound to consider.

Denotation: What is the exact meaning of the word? This is the definition you will find in the dictionary.

Connotation: What meanings does this word suggest beyond its exact meaning? What is the emotive quality of this word? For example, the word "cancer" means a disease characterized by the abnormal growth of cells. Emotionally, the word "cancer" conjures up fear, terror, worry, helplessness, etc. Words often have such connotative connections and we need to be aware of them when we use them.

SOUND

Poems are meant to be heard. It has been said that poetry is language that "drips from the tongue." We must pay attention to the sound of language as well as to the meaning of language. Sound, when used intentionally, should always enhance or reinforce meaning. You will not be asked to identify particular sound patterns, meter or rhyme on the exam. However, there are times when the sound of a poem contributes heavily to meaning. For example, musicality is connected to tone. Any shifts in sound are also worth noting.

Sound elements:

Rhyme: words that sound either exactly alike or merely similar. The word "rhyme" is sometimes seen as "rime," particularly in archaic texts.

Exact rhyme:

▶ cat, hat, flat, mat: *masculine rhyme (one syllable rhymes)*

▶ falling, calling, stalling: *feminine rhyme (two or more syllables rhyme)*

Slant rhyme/approximate rhyme:

▶ *the words sound close but are not exact rhymes*

▶ mirror, steer, dear *or* book, crack, stick *(consonance is used most often for slant rhymes).*

Internal rhyme vs. end rhyme: end rhyme occurs only at the end of the line whereas internal rhyme happens within a line

Alliteration: repetition of beginning sounds in close proximity: "Susan sent Sally some sunflowers," or "Loons lurk late in autumn lakes under lavender skies."

Assonance: repetition of vowel sounds: *cake, stake, break, fate, drank, ache, placate,* etc. Some words using assonance will rhyme exactly: others will simply mirror the vowel sounds.

Cacophony: harsh, discordant, or unpleasing sounds

Consonance: repetition of consonant sounds: exact rhymes use consonance: *foot, put, soot.* But any words that repeat consonant sounds are using consonance: add suit, unfit, and unlit to the preceding list. The key is that they all end with the "t" sound. Consonance can occur in the middle of words also: *river, liver, cadaver, palaver, waver, save, rave,* etc. The "v" sound repeats.

Euphony: pleasing, melodious, pleasant sounds

Meter: a rhythm accomplished by using a certain number of beats or syllables per line: the most common form of meter is iambic meter which is a foot consisting of one unstressed syllable followed by a stressed syllable represented like this: (‿ /). A foot is simply two syllables (or in some cases, three) that form a metrical pattern. Iambs are common in everyday English; iambic pentameter means a five-foot iambic line, or ten syllables.

Sound should never be more important than the idea or meaning of the poem, but should always work to extend the meaning of the poem.

Sound is less likely to be a significant factor in construing meaning in older, fixed form poems. Poets prior to the 19th century were not considered to have mastered their craft if they could not control rhyme schemes and metrical patterns. Free verse poets since the mid-1800s and beyond felt less constrained by form and rigid meter, so they were free to experiment more liberally with sound. For these poets, sound is something to mold, play with, and use to enhance their ideas.

Test Tip

You will not be asked to identify rhyme schemes or other poetic patterns on the exam. However, you might make the case that a rhyme scheme contributes to an overall tone in a poem. Sound does impact meaning.

METAPHOR

A metaphor is a comparison of two dissimilar things to help us see something in a new or more meaningful way. Similes are also metaphors, but use the words "like" or "as" in making the comparison. "Life is like a river" is a simile.

Besides the simile, there are two basic types of metaphor:

Direct metaphor: the comparison is made directly using the word "is." "Life is a river."

Indirect metaphor: "The river of life" also compares life to a river but does so indirectly.

Comparison is one of our basic patterns of reasoning. We perceive the world and compare new things/experiences to what we already know to see how they are alike or different and in this process, we make judgments and understand ideas.

There are other ways of comparing:

Personification: giving something non-human, human characteristics. A tree could be compared to a human being, which may help readers feel empathy for a tree.

Oxymoron: juxtaposing two things apparently contradictory that still reinforce one idea—jumbo shrimp, only choice, virtual reality.

Hyperbole: using exaggeration to extend reality. Hyperbole gets us to look more closely at what is actually true by giving us a sharp contrast.

Understatement: this works in the opposite way from hyperbole. We use understatement when we intentionally minimize something's importance to create an ironic or rhetorical effect.

THEME

Why write poems? Some people can't help it. Writing poetry is as natural to them as breathing and it's not a choice—they just do it. Still, there must be some reason beyond the process itself for writing poems. We could say that the poem's theme or central idea is the poet's purpose. It's what the poet needed to say. Themes express the unity of human experience, and through poems we see that we are more alike as a human race than different.

Themes express the poet's vision—the artist's vision about the truth of the world. Some common themes are love, hate, hunger, growing up, growing old, dying, fears, cruelty, compassion, etc. A theme in a poem can be found in an epic tale or a simple reflection: both light the way to understanding.

SAYING SOMETHING NEW OR
SAYING SOMETHING OLD IN A NEW WAY

Poetry is one of the oldest art forms, and poets have pretty much covered all there is to say. Still, we all are constantly reinventing ourselves and our world and we can say something new, or at least something old in a new way. As beginning poets, we learn sometimes through imitating the great poems we admire. This is a good and natural way to learn. But we cannot imitate forever. At some point, we must find our own voices and we must allow them to say the things that "we know." "What you know that I don't know is what you can tell me in a poem," the poet Sharon Olds said. "After all, what else is there? I cannot write about anything else. I can only tell you what I know."

This is a tricky thing, though. Sometimes we think we know things through our own experiences that we really don't—what we do is try to appropriate vicarious experience for our poems. Young poets may take a life lived on TV or in a movie and write about it as if it were their own. Ideas for poems can come through the observed lives of others—but what matters is what we know about that experience and this knowledge comes only from our own experience—from our own learning. This is what Olds meant: this is what we know.

Saying something old in a new way can mean using new forms, new ideas in language, infusing the truly new world of science/ technology/reality with the very, very old questions of humanity. It's all about perception: how do you see the world? What can you say about it that hasn't already been said?

Poems on the AP exam are likely chosen for several reasons:

- complexity of language and idea
- particular use of figurative language
- a view of life that is unique or startling
- *likely all of the above*

KEY TERMS

Familiarize yourself with the following list of terms. The starred terms (★) are those that have appeared more prominently on released AP Lit exams.

1. **alliteration**: repetition, at close intervals, of beginning sounds.

2. ★ **apostrophe**: a speaker directly addresses something or someone not living, as a lady in a tapestry, or the wind.

3. **assonance**: repetition at close intervals of vowel sounds. At its most basic, assonance is simple rhyme (*cat, hat*). Assonance provides a fluency of sound.

4. **consonance**: repetition at close intervals of consonant sounds, such as *book, plaque, thicker*.

5. **couplet**: two lines that rhyme. Shakespearean sonnets end with a couplet. Set apart, couplets may contain a separate or complete idea. Sometimes a couplet can serve as a stanza.

6. ★ **epigraph**: a short quotation or verse that precedes a poem (or any text) that sets a tone, provides a setting, or gives some other context for the poem.

7. **fixed form (closed form)**: some poems have a fixed form, meaning that there are "rules" about numbers of lines, meter, rhyme schemes, etc. See a list of common fixed-form poems later in this chapter.

8. **iambic pentameter**: a line of five iambic feet, or ten syllables. See the section on Meter later in this chapter.

9. ★ **imagery**: language that appeals to the senses and evokes emotion.

10. ★ **metaphor**: a comparison of two unlike things in order to show something new. A basic metaphor contains a literal term (the thing being compared) and a figurative term (the thing the literal term is being compared with).

11. **metaphysical conceit**: an elaborate, intellectually ingenious metaphor that shows the poet's realm of knowledge; it may be brief or extended.

12. ★ **meter**: the rhythmic pattern of poetry. See the section on meter later in this chapter.

13. ★ **personification**: to personify is to attribute human qualities or characteristics to nonliving things. To attribute human qualities to animals is called **anthropomorphism**.

14. **pun**: a play on words where the juxtaposition of meanings is ironic or humorous.

15. **rhyme (internal rhyme)**: words that rhyme within a line of poetry.

16. **rhyme (rhyme scheme)**: a regular pattern of end rhymes. To mark a rhyme scheme, label the first line "a," the next line if it does not rhyme with the first "b," and so on. Certain fixed form poems, like sonnets, have specific rhyme schemes.

17. **rhythm**: the beat or music of a poem. A regular beat indicates a metrical pattern.

18. **sestet**: a stanza of six lines. See other stanza types below.

19. **simile**: a metaphor that uses comparison words such as "like" or "as." An **epic simile** or **Homeric simile** (named after Homer) is an elaborate simile that compares an ordinary event or situation (familiar to the audience) with the idea in the text. These similes are often recognized by the "just as, so then" construction. Dante Alighieri makes extensive use of epic similes.

20. ★ **speaker**: the narrative voice of a poem. A poem generally has only one speaker, but some poems may have more than one. In a poetry analysis you would not refer to the "narrator" but instead the "speaker."

21. ★ **stanza**: the "paragraph" of a poem, whether consisting of equal or unequal numbers of lines. **Stanzaic form** refers to a poem that has stanzas. A poem without stanzas is a **continuous form** poem.

22. ★ **structure**: the way the poem is built, such as three stanzas of terza rima, or one stanza (continuous form) of successive couplets.

23. **synechdoche** (pronounced sin-**eck**-doe-key, emphasis on second syllable): the use of a part for the whole, such as "all hands on deck"

24. ★ **tone**: the emotional quality of a poem, such as regretful or contemplative. Tone also refers to the speaker's attitude (feelings about) a particular thing or idea.

25. **unity**: the degree to which elements of a poem work together to produce a coherent effect

Test Tip

Remember to pay attention to stanza shifts. A new stanza may present a new idea or theme or a shift in tone.

HOW TO READ A POEM

As you learned above, a poem is often full of figurative language, which means you shouldn't read a poem for its literal sense though there will be literal elements in the poem. What I mean is, you have to be open to surprises in poems. Good poets get us to feel before we think, and often we must read poems several times to get meaning from them.

It is possible to misread a poem. Sometimes students say that a poem can mean whatever you want it to mean, sort of like looking at an abstract painting and interpreting it however you like. However, you are not allowed to ignore the context of the poem when making your interpretation. A poem is a small thing, generally. Each word has been chosen carefully and it should have a purpose. You cannot simply notice some words and ignore others. If there is a word in a poem you don't understand, you have to look it up. This is different from reading a novel, where missing a word now and again makes very little difference.

Below is a simple method for reading a poem for analytical purposes. Putting this method into practice should help you feel more confident, both in reading poetry and understanding it.

1. **Read** the poem

   ‣ *Read slowly and, if possible, out loud. Subvocalizing is the process of reading out loud in one's head. The best way to read a poem is to really verbalize it, to give it actual sound.*

   ‣ *Read meaningful chunks, not lines. If there is punctuation, use it. If not, find discrete chunks of meaning (phrases and clauses). In other words, you do not necessarily stop at the end of each line. You stop at the end of a line if there is a period; you pause if there is a comma. If there is no punctuation, you may just keep reading onto the next line.*

   ‣ *Be very careful of rhythmic poems that have a beat; you can lose your quest for meaning if you get caught up in the "music." However, the music might be a clue to the poet's theme, so keep it in mind.*

2. **Annotate** the poem for **STIFS** (see Chapter 10 for a sample annotated poem)

S = Speaker

▸ *Identify the speaker and any particular character traits of the speaker (especially his or her point of view).*

▸ *Who is the speaker addressing?*

▸ *What is the speaker's topic, argument, etc.*

T = Tone

▸ *What is the dominant tone in the poem?*

▸ *Is there a shift in tone? If so, where is it and why do you think the shift occurs?*

I = Imagery

▸ *Isolate the major images: what do you see, smell, hear, taste, feel?*

▸ *What is suggested by the imagery? Emotion? Idea?*

F = Figurative Language

▸ *Find and understand the figurative language evident in the poem: metaphor, simile, apostrophe, personification, hyperbole, and more.*

▸ *Determine what's really being said in each instance of figurative language. Moreover, determine how the metaphor or other figure of speech is related to other elements or details in the poem and/or how it functions in the poem as a whole.*

S = Sound

▸ *What sound elements are most striking and why? You should be looking for sound repetition, cacophony/euphony, or any element of sound that reinforces meaning.*

3. **Read** the poem again after you've annotated it.

4. If you are stuck on particular phrases, that is, if you don't understand them, make sure you have defined all complex language and then paraphrase the tricky parts. By simplifying the language in clauses and phrases, it will be easier for you to understand the basic idea.

5. **Answer this question:** What is this poem about and how do I know this? Be sure you can support your claims with evidence from the poem. Look to your annotations for your evidence.

Test Tip

Understanding Shakespeare can be difficult. You might find it helpful to study smaller passages, such as sonnets, and paraphrase them until you get the knack of Elizabethan language.

METER

Meter is the regular pattern of accented and unaccented syllables in a poem.

You will not be asked to identify a particular metrical pattern on the exam. This section is included to clarify any questions you may have about meter.

Meter is marked by stressed (/) and unstressed (u) syllables. A metrical foot consists of either two syllables per foot (duple meter) or three syllables per foot (triple meter). The most common meter is iambic, a duple meter. The most common measure is iambic pentameter, which is found throughout Shakespeare's works.

TYPES OF METER

Type	Adjective Form	Syllable pattern
iamb	iambic	U /
trochee	trochaic	/ U
anapest	anapestic	U U /
dactyl	dactylic	/ / U
spondee	spondaic	/ /

MEASURES OF METER

monometer	One foot
dimeter	Two feet
trimeter	Three feet

STANZA TYPES

couplet	two-line stanza
tercet	three-line stanza
quatrain	four-line stanza
quintain	five-line stanza
sestet	six-line stanza
septet	seven-line stanza
octave	eight-line stanza

COMMON FIXED FORM POEMS

Haiku: Haiku is a traditional Japanese fixed-form poem. It is structured in three lines, with five syllables in the first, seven syllables in the second, and five syllables in the third. One intention of haiku is to capture a moment in time or a perceived aspect of nature.

Sestina: A sestina is a complicated French form of poetry traditionally consisting of six six-line stanzas followed by a tercet, called an "envoy," to equal 39 lines in all. A set of six words is repeated in varying patterns at the ends of the lines of each of the six-line stanzas. These six words also appear in the envoy, two in each line of the tercet.

Sonnet: You may have heard the phrase, "If it's square, it's a sonnet." A sonnet is fourteen lines of iambic pentameter, generally with either of two traditional rhyme schemes: Shakespearean/English: ABAB CDCD EFEF GG (three quatrains followed by a rhyming couplet); or Petrarchan/Italian: ABBAABBA CDECDE an octave (two quatrains) presenting a problem followed by a sestet (two tercets) giving the solution. Or, the sestet signals a change in tone or other shift.

Villanelle: This fixed-form poem consists of 19 lines composed of five tercets (rhyme scheme: aba) and a concluding quatrain (rhyme scheme: abaa). Lines one and three of the first tercet serve as refrains in a pattern that alternates through line 15. This pattern is repeated again in lines 18 and 19. The most famous example of a villanelle is Dylan Thomas's poem, *Do Not Go Gentle Into That Good Night*.

OTHER TYPES OF POEMS

1. **Ballad**: a short poem in song format (sometimes with refrains) that tells a story

2. **Elegy**: a poem, the subject of which is the death of a person or, in some cases, an idea

3. **Epic**: long, adventurous tale with a hero, generally on a quest

4. **Lyric**: expresses love, inner emotions, tends to be personal; usually written in first person

5. **Narrative**: the poet tells a story with characters and a plot

6. **Ode**: Originally a Greek form, odes are serious lyric poems. There are a variety of types of odes. English Romantic poets reinvigorated the form.

7. **Prose poem**: a prose poem looks like a paragraph, even having a jagged right margin. It may even read like a paragraph, but it retains poetic elements such as imagery, figurative language, and concise diction.

TWENTY "MUST READ" POEMS

There are thousands of great poems and hundreds of great poets. This list is meant only to acquaint you with some standard poems that AP Lit students often study. But please, do go beyond this list. Embrace poems and they will cease to frighten you. The following poems are in no particular order. They are examples of old, new, British, and American poems. Each one should be easy to find in a good college literature anthology, and many may even be online.

Go beyond just reading these poems. Study them. Use the analytical reading method found earlier in this chapter. The list below offers you a wide variety of forms, themes, and examples of poetic elements. Most of the poems below are well known by AP English Literature teachers, so if you're stumped by any of them, seek a teacher's help.

1. *My Last Duchess*, Robert Browning

2. *The Lovesong of J. Alfred Prufrock*, T.S. Eliot

3. *Ozymandias*, Percy Bysshe Shelley

4. *A Valediction: Forbidding Mourning,* John Donne (or anything by Donne)

5. *Out, Out—,* Robert Frost

6. *Dover Beach,* Matthew Arnold

7. *Bells for John Whiteside's Daughter,* John Crowe Ransom

8. *The Second Coming,* William Butler Yeats

9. *Dulce et Decorum Est,* Wilfred Owen

10. *I felt a Funeral, in my Brain,* Emily Dickinson

11. *Those Winter Sundays,* Robert Hayden

12. *To His Coy Mistress,* Andrew Marvell

13. *The Weary Blues,* Langston Hughes

14. *Woman Work,* Maya Angelou

15. *Do Not Go Gentle Into That Good Night,* Dylan Thomas

16. *In the Waiting Room,* Elizabeth Bishop

17. *Ode on a Grecian Urn,* John Keats

18. *Sunday Morning,* Wallace Stevens

19. *The Colonel,* Carolyn Forché

20. Any Shakespearean sonnet

Test Tip

The internet can be a great source of information regarding classic poetry. The Poetry Foundation, publishers of Poetry magazine, has published poem guides for some of the poems in this list (as well as other great poems to study). Why not check it out: **https://www.poetryfoundation.org/articles/category/poem-guides.**

Rhetoric and Grammar

OVERVIEW

The purpose of this chapter is to give you a basic understanding of rhetoric and why it is important on the AP Lit exam. The AP English Language and Composition exam is the full-fledged test of your rhetorical skills, but there are some questions on the AP English Literature and Composition exam that have to do with argument and persuasion. Of course, the essays you write for the AP Literature exam require your best rhetorical skills. The terms and concepts in this chapter focus on the uses of language, aspects of argument, and elements of linguistic style.

WHAT IS RHETORIC?

Rhetoric is the use of language to persuade. In more general terms, rhetoric is the effective use of language for a variety of purposes. If you intend to study for the AP English Language and Composition exam, you will become much more intimately familiar with rhetoric and rhetorical devices. For now, though, it is enough to recognize a few basic aspects. If you have already taken the AP English Language exam, this chapter will be a good review.

On the AP English Literature exam, you are likely to be presented with an argument from a variety of genres: essay, poem, narrative prose, even an excerpt from a novel. For example, a poet may argue that time is short, so it is best to love while we can, as in Andrew Marvell's poem *To His Coy Mistress*. Marvell's poem is an excellent example of a highly structured argument in poetic form.

A variety of questions regarding rhetoric are typically found on the AP Lit exam. Some common types are listed below:

- The question asks you to determine the primary rhetorical effect, purpose, or function of a passage or section.

- The question asks you to identify the central rhetorical strategy used in the passage. See more on rhetorical strategies below.

- The question asks you to determine the purpose, function, or rhetorical purpose of a sentence, phrase, clause, or word.

- The question asks you to determine the effect of a rhetorical shift.

KEY TERMS

1. **abstraction**: a concept or idea without a specific example; idealized generalities

2. **abstract noun**: ideas or things that can mean many things to many people, such as peace, honor, etc.

3. **analogy**: compares two situations that are similar in several respects in order to prove a point or clarify an idea

4. **antecedent**: that which comes before; the antecedent of a pronoun is the noun to which the referent pronoun refers (you may be expected to find this relationship in a passage)

5. **antithesis**: the opposite of an idea used to emphasize a point; the juxtaposition of contrasting words or ideas. Example: *To err is human; to forgive, divine.*

6. **catalog (list):** Walt Whitman used catalogs or lists of like elements in his poems; lists of details can reinforce a concept. Inductive arguments build to a conclusion based on the collective impression of lists (facts).

7. **circumlocution**: to write around a subject; to write evasively; to say nothing

8. **double entendre:** a phrase or saying that has two meanings, one being sexual or provocative in nature

9. **ethos:** a speaker or writer's credibility; his or her character, honesty, commitment to the writing

10. **euphemism:** a kinder, gentler, less crude or harsh word or phrase to replace one that seems imprudent to use in a particular situation

11. **hyperbole:** an exaggeration or overstatement— saying more than is warranted by the situation in order to expose reality by comparison; also, one of the main techniques in satire

12. **juxtapose (juxtaposition):** to place side by side in order to show similarities or differences

13. **lists:** see catalog

14. **oxymoron:** a figure of speech in which two contradictory elements are combined for effect, such as "deafening silence"

15. **paradox:** the juxtaposition of incongruous or conflicting ideas that reveal a truth or insight

16. **parallel structure**: equal or similar grammatical or rhetorical elements used side by side or in succession, generally for emphasis

17. **parody**: a humorous imitation of an original text meant to ridicule, used as a technique in satire

18. **pathos:** the quality in literature that appeals to the audience's emotions

19. **repetition**: any of a variety of devices that emphasize through repetition: one example of a repetition device is *anaphora*, which is the repetition of the same word or words at the beginning of successive phrases, clauses, or sentences

20. **rhetoric**: the use of language for persuasion (in our context, persuasive writing)

21. **rhetorical strategy**: various strategies and appeals that writers use to persuade. The main appeals are to logic/reason, to needs, to tradition, to emotion, and to ethics/fairness.

22. **satire**: type of literature that exposes idiocy, corruption, or other human folly through humor, exaggeration, and irony

23. **understatement**: saying less than is warranted by the situation in order to emphasize reality

24. **verb phrase**: the verb and its object and modifiers

25. **vernacular**: the ordinary, everyday speech of a region

BASIC RHETORICAL STRATEGIES

Entire books have been written on this subject, but you don't have the time or the need to read one of those. Instead, know these basic strategies and you will do well.

BASIC APPEALS:

A writer can appeal to readers'

- **needs** (hierarchy of needs: shelter, esteem, etc.)
- **sense of tradition** (we've always done it this way)
- **ethics** (sense of fairness, right or wrong)
- **emotions** (pull at the heartstrings)
- **logic/reason** (suggest what is logical and support it with a reasoned argument)

There are also appeals to

- **authority** (stating facts, expert opinion, statistics)
- **shared values** (success, freedom, equality, etc.)

STYLISTIC DEVICES EFFECTIVE WRITERS USE:

- evocative or emotive language
- lists of relevant details
- figurative language, especially to get readers to see things in a fresh way
- imagery, appeals to senses and draws readers into the text
- repetition, used for emphasis
- parallel structure, used for emphasis
- irony, points out flaws and reveals the truth
- analogy, shows logical relationships

MODES/FORMS OF RHETORIC

- cause and effect
- problem and solution

- narrative
- description
- definition
- humor
- satire

THE VERBS OF RHETORIC

The questions and prompts in the AP Lit exam are loaded with a variety of meaningful verbs. It is important to know what each means, as subtle differences may be important in understanding a question or your task.

Allege: to assert but without proof; allegations require proof

Analyze: to break apart; to look at component parts of a text in order to understand an aspect of the whole

Argue: to defend a claim, to provide evidence for an assertion

Assert: to formally declare as true

Broach: to bring up a topic for discussion

Characterize: to depict something in a certain way; to give specific characteristics of someone or something

Claim: to make a statement of "fact," something you intend to prove

Clarify: to draw distinctions, to make more evident, to lessen confusion

Discuss: to consider in writing a variety of possible views (ways of interpretation) on a topic

Dramatize: to give a story to a situation, to add vivid details, such as imagery, figurative language, etc.

Emphasize: to give added importance or weight to something

Establish: to set a foundation for, to base a claim on an observation

Imply: to state indirectly; to have a logical consequence

Indicate: to be a signal of; to state or express

Observe: to take notice of, and thereby, it is implied, to draw conclusions

Paraphrase: to put into more common, less complex (or technical) language

Propose: to suggest a plan or a solution to a problem

Rebuff: to reject

Suggest: to offer a perspective, a solution, a way of thinking about something for consideration

Support: to provide evidence and give reasons and examples for a statement of fact or a claim

A QUESTION OF GRAMMAR

The AP Lit exam is not a grammar test. It is a literary analysis test. However, your ability to control the conventions of good writing is expected. Also, you will typically encounter a few questions that ask about relationships between words or parts of sentences. These types of questions test your ability to read and comprehend complex poetry and prose.

Examples:

1. The question asks you to identify what a phrase or clause modifies.

2. The question asks you to make a grammatical connection, such as "The word or phrase refers to . . ."

3. The question asks you to find a word's antecedent.

Hopefully, none of the terms in the preceding questions elude you, but if so, here are some definitions.

PHRASE:

- A phrase is a group of related words that does not contain a subject and verb. There are a variety of phrase types, but it is unlikely that you will be asked to identify phrase types.

CLAUSE:

- An independent clause is also called a main clause or, more commonly, a sentence. An independent clause has a subject and a verb and can stand independently.

- A subordinate or dependent clause has either a subject or a verb and cannot stand independently.

MODIFIES:

- *Modifies* means to add meaning to, such as adjectives modifying nouns (*blue* dress) or adverbs modifying verbs (walked *slowly*)

ANTECEDENT:

- *Antecedent* means that which comes before. Referents have antecedents. "Laura found her hat on the top shelf." "Laura" is the antecedent of the referent "her."

The AP Lit exam also tests your ability to write complex or sophisticated prose when writing your essays. When you write, you'll need to consider the types of sentences and how you vary them, the vocabulary you use, including the kinds of verbs you use, and much more. See Chapter 15 for tips on writing well.

Mastering Difficult Vocabulary

"Too many students do not possess the vocabulary and do not understand the various nuances of language to be able to read imaginative literature."

—The College Board

OVERVIEW

The following words were chosen from AP Lit released exams because they are generally difficult, may be archaic in meaning, or have a specific cultural meaning.

The purpose of this list is not to imply that these words will show up on future exams, but to suggest that in order for you to confidently deal with complex texts, you need to have a fairly extensive vocabulary, not just words you know the meanings of, but words you are comfortable using in a variety of contexts.

Rather than memorize the following list of words and meanings, your time is better spent understanding difficult words you encounter in the texts you are reading, either by using contextual clues to determine meaning or by looking them up in a dictionary (or better yet, both). However, this list can enhance your study, so do review it often if you have time.

In order to further your vocabulary skills, a section on Greek and Latin roots (etymons) is included at the end of this chapter. Knowing root parts of words can really amp up your ability to determine word meanings in context.

Test Tip

When you are confronted with a word you don't know on the exam, try to determine the meaning from context clues. If that does not work, it might be safe to ignore the word and focus on the overall meaning of the passage. Keep in mind, though, in poetry each word matters more than in prose passages. Either way, attempting to get the general idea is always your goal.

VOCABULARY LIST

1. **adamantine** (adj): (from the noun adamant, which is a hard, crystallized carbon) firm in attitude or opinion, unyielding (contemporary usage: adamant, meaning firm, unyielding)

2. **admonish** (verb): to scold, censor

3. **amorphous** (adj): without shape or form

4. **animal husbandry** (noun): the practice of breeding and raising livestock (also called animal science)

5. **apostles** (noun): the 12 men who were Jesus's early followers, or disciples. More broadly, they are advocates sent to deliver or spread teachings to others.

6. **austere** (adj)/**austerity** (noun): severe or stern in disposition or appearance, having great self-denial (materialistically)

7. **bade** (verb): to order, to instruct

8. **belies** (verb): contradicts

9. **bellicose** (adj): loud, argumentative, prone to fighting

10. **benign** (adj): harmless

11. **bosom** (noun): the chest, typically a woman's and place of warmth and love

12. **chaste** (adj): pure, virginal

13. **chasten** (verb): to chastise, castigate, correct

14. **couch, couched** (verb): to word in a certain manner

15. **cultivate** (verb): to grow, to nurture

16. **curate, curates** (noun): a clergyman; (verb): to direct or manage a museum or an exhibit

17. **damask** (noun): a fabric of linen, cotton, silk, or wool with a reversible pattern woven into it

18. **degenerate** (verb): to degrade or lessen in value; (noun): a morally bankrupt person, a profligate

19. **deity** (noun): a god

20. **din** (noun): loud, raucous noise

21. **dumb** (adj): mute, unable to speak

22. **effeminate** (adj): having feminine qualities, generally only used to describe men

23. **eminent** (adj)/**eminence** (noun): distinguished, having high stature

24. **emulate** (verb): to imitate or copy (as with a role model)

25. entreat (verb)/entreaty (noun): to beg/begging

26. equinox (noun): either of two times of the year when the sun crosses the plane of the earth's equator and day and night are of equal length

27. facility (noun)/facile (adj): adeptness/with ease

28. faculty (noun): ability, power

29. homage (noun): respect, honor

30. hutch (noun): a cupboard for dishes or accommodation for rabbits

31. impervious (adj): not able to be penetrated

32. impious (adj): irreverent

33. indefatigable (adj): inability to tire, tireless

34. indict (verb)/indictment (noun): to charge, to accuse/a charge or accusation

35. inherent (adj)/inherently (adverb): integral, intrinsic/in an inherent manner

36. jocund (adj): merry, mirthful, gay

37. languor (noun): state of ease, rest, even listlessness

38. lentils (noun): small split pea-like legumes

39. lethargic (adj): tired, listless

40. lore (noun): traditional knowledge, passed on through fables, stories, etc.

41. mien (noun): bearing, presence, manner

42. naivete (noun)/naïve (adj): innocence, inexperience

43. nascent (adj): emerging, newly born or created

44. ordain (verb): to appoint to a clerical post (minister, priest) or to order due to superior authority

45. parody (verb or noun): to spoof, to mock; a parody is a text meant to spoof or mock (a form of satire)

46. phenomenon (noun): a remarkable development

47. piety (noun): righteousness, godliness

48. plight (noun): predicament, quandary, difficulty

49. pretense (noun): deception, deceit

50. primeval (adj): aboriginal, primordial, primal (first)

51. prodigy (noun): genius, especially a gifted child

52. proffer (verb): to suggest, to propose

53. profundity (noun): intellectual depth; penetrating knowledge; keen insight; etc.

54. promulgate (verb): to proclaim or exclaim

55. prowess (noun): special skill

56. quarry (noun): prey, victim; also a pit where gravel or ore is mined

57. raiment (noun): especially fine or decorative clothing

58. reap (verb): to gather, glean, harvest

59. reticent (adj)/reticence (noun): shyness, unwillingness

60. rheumatism (noun): painful disorder of the joints or muscles or connective tissues

61. sable (noun): as a color, dark, black-brown, fur from the animal sable

62. scourge (noun): bane, curse, affliction or a whip or lash used to inflict punishment

63. sepulcher (noun): burial chamber, tomb

64. sire (noun and verb): a father; to father, engender

65. supine (adj): lying prone, flat, especially in humility

66. **suppliant** (verb and noun): to petition or beseech, one who begs for intercession

67. **surplice** (noun): a loose-fitting white ecclesiastical vestment with wide sleeves

68. **temper, tempered** (verb): toughen (steel or glass) by a process of gradually heating and cooling

69. **timorous** (adj): timid, fearful, apprehensive

70. **tinged** (adj): slightly touched with

71. **tumult** (noun): **tumultuous** (adj): uproar, disturbance

72. **vehement** (adj)/**vehemence** (noun): marked by extreme intensity of emotions or convictions; inclined to react violently

73. **veracity** (noun): truthfulness

74. **vocation** (noun): a calling, such as the ministry; a job one seems meant to do.

75. **whorl** (noun): swirl, ringlet, curlicue

Make learning new words a game. When you learn a new word, commit to using it at least ten times in one day in a variety of contexts. Bonus: You might have fun annoying those around you!

GREEK AND LATIN ROOTS

At some point you will need to determine the meaning of unfamiliar words from context clues. If you have a working knowledge of some basic Greek and Latin prefixes and roots, you can often quickly decipher word meanings, particularly when words are scientific in nature. Perhaps you've learned many of these roots in a science or world language class. If so, concentrate on those in this list that are new to you. This list is by no means complete, but it does contain a good sampling of roots that will aid your decoding skills.

For fun, take note of the English examples below that contain more than one of the roots. *Autograph*, for example, means "self-write."

Root/Prefix	Meaning	English Examples
ab-, a-, abs-	away, from	abstain, absent
ante-	before	anteroom, antecedent, antebellum
anthrop-	human	anthropomorphic, misanthrope
anti-	against	antidote, antipathy
auto-	self	autobiography, autoimmune, autocratic
bell-	war	bellicose, belligerent
bene-	good	benevolent, beneficiary, beneficial
bi-	two	biennial, bisect, bicycle
bio	life	biology, biosphere, biogenesis
-cede	go, yield, surrender	concede, recede
circum-	around	circumference, circumlocution
con-	with	conspire, connect
contra-	against	contraband, contrary, contrast
de-	down, from	devolve, decline, devoid
dic-, dict-, dit-	say, speak	diction, dictate
dis-, di-	apart, away	dissolve, dissuade, diverge, divest

Continued →

(Continued from previous page)

Root/Prefix	Meaning	English Examples
ex-, e-	out of, from	eject, emerge, extricate, example
-fid, -fide, -feder	faith, trust	confide, bona fide, fidelity
graph-, gram-	write, draw	graphic, telegram, autograph
hyper-	beyond, over	hyperbole, hyperactive
hypo-	under, less	hypodermic, hypocrite
inter-	among, between	interstate, intercede, introspection
intra-	within	intramural, intravenous
log-, logo-, -ology	reason, learning	logistics, catalog
loqu-, locut-	talk, speak	eloquent, colloquial, loquacious
mal-	bad, evil	malnourished, malinger
mis-	ill, mistaken, wrong	misunderstood, misogyny
morph-	shape, form	amorphic, metamorphosis
para-, par-	beside	paralegal, parameter
phil-	love	philosophy, philanthropic
post-	after, following	postpone, postgraduate
pre-	before	precursor, preface, premonition
pro-	forward, outward	project, protract
soph-	wisdom	sophomore, sophist
super-	above	superior, superimpose
tele-, tel-	far	television, telekinesis, telemarketer

Root/Prefix	Meaning	English Examples
trans-	across	transpose, transcontinental, transgender
-vert	turn	revert, convert, introvert
vid-, vis-	to see	visual, video, envision
viv-, vita-, vivi-	alive, life	vivacious, vitality, vivid
vol-	will, wish	malevolent, voluntary

Test Tip

Review practice exams for troublesome vocabulary, particularly words that caused you to answer incorrectly because you did not know their meanings. Add these to the list below.

MY OWN VOCABULARY LIST

In Chapter 10, "Engaged and Active Reading," you are encouraged to annotate texts as you read and circle words that you don't know. You may want to add those words here, and look them up to help you increase your working vocabulary.

	Word	Definition
1.		
2.		
3.		
4.		
5.		

Continued →

(Continued from previous page)

Word	Definition
6.	
7.	
8.	
9.	
10.	
11.	
12.	
13.	
14.	
15.	
16.	
17.	
18.	
19.	
20.	

PART III:

INTERPRETING READING PASSAGES

Engaged and Active Reading

IMPROVING READING HABITS

In the multiple-choice section of the AP Lit exam, you will have 60 minutes to carefully read five to six texts—a combination of fictional prose, essay, and poetry—and answer approximately 55 questions on those texts (see Chapter 19). In the essay section, you will have two texts to read—generally a poem and a prose passage. If you don't fully understand what you've read, you will not be able to write intelligent essays.

In either case, you will not have time for leisurely reading. However, you still must be able to read actively and reflectively with all your faculties engaged. You may only have time to read each text once, so you must read carefully and with purpose.

A quick assessment of your reading skills can prove enlightening. Your reading habits may need a makeover if any of the following rings true for you:

- You find yourself thinking of something else about every other sentence.

- You have to reread a paragraph about five times to know what it means.

- You have to look up definitions for many words.

- You are bored by the passage so you just skim through it, but then you have no idea what it is about.

- You sometimes characterize the text as "stupid," "dumb," "pointless," etc.

Some of the problems listed above have to do with **your attitude** about the reading. It is fair to say that not all the passages and poems on the AP Lit exam will be to your liking, but it will be important for you to control your negative emotional response. Negative emotions will interfere with your motivation and will cloud your ability to think clearly. The fix? Approach each passage as something you can *mostly* understand. You aren't expected to be an *expert* on any of the texts on the exam. Instead, you are being tested on your ability to read critically and analytically.

If you find yourself rereading often, you may actually be reading too slowly—allowing distracting outside thoughts into your head. This is a matter of **concentration** and it is something you can control. Before exam day, practice reading complex texts at a rate faster than you would normally read—not so fast that you are skimming the text—but quickly enough to force concentration on the text, which will minimize those pesky outside thoughts. (This strategy works, but it isn't an instant fix. With practice, you will see improved concentration.)

MORE STRATEGIES FOR IMPROVING YOUR READING

BE HYPERCONSCIOUS

- Make a conscious effort to understand what you're doing as you read. As soon as your mind starts wandering, toss out a mental lasso and pull yourself back. Work on keeping your focus.

IMPROVE STAMINA

- If you start to get tired, drink water, not energy drinks, and remember to breathe steadily. Do some neck exercises to get your blood circulating to your brain. You won't be allowed to get up and walk around during the exam, so try to get used to reading, concentrating, and thinking for periods of an hour or more at a time.

BE COMFORTABLE

- Let your body help you read. Your text should be in line with your sight. Your visual path can't bend. Prop up your book—don't lay it flat on a desk or table. And your arms will get tired if you try to hold a book up while lying flat on the floor or in bed. Practice your reading while sitting at a desk or a table, as this is the most likely position you'll be in while taking the AP exam.

MINIMIZE DISTRACTIONS

- Do NOT read while listening to music! You may think you are concentrating, but, in reality, you are forcing your brain to think of two things at once, a practice that is stressful and counterproductive for exam prep. You will not be allowed to have any electronic devices (including smartphones) with you for the exam, so get used to reading in relative silence.

CONTROL BIASES AND EMOTIONS

- Practice controlling your emotions by choosing some tough texts to read. Read them, annotate them, and feel good about your progress. Read Shakespeare, Jane Austen, Voltaire, or Dostoevsky, to start.

SELECT PRACTICE TEXTS

- A lot of older texts are online. You can download them to an e-reader, or read them online. If you really want to practice annotating the text, it is best to have paper copies of the texts. You can search Project Gutenberg (http://www.gutenberg.org), for example, to find many of the authors listed in Chapters 3 and 4.

Test Tip

Classic works of literature are often inexpensive. Why not invest in two or three? Studies show that people who read paper books remember what they read better than those who read digital books. Plus, you can write in your own book, which is a huge advantage.

READ STRATEGICALLY

- Give yourself permission to skip words. You don't have to read every single word to know what's going on. This is not to say that you should skim—not at all, but if you think you have to look up every word, you will miss the "big picture." This is especially true of novels, plays, or longer works. However, this tip does not apply to poetry. Because there are so few words in a poem, each one is important.

ANNOTATE TEXTS

- Learn how to annotate texts and practice this skill before the exam. This may be the most important thing you can do to improve your reading skills for the AP Lit exam. There is more on this later in this chapter.

READ WITH PURPOSE

- When you take your AP Lit exam, plan to quickly skim the multiple-choice questions that relate to a text. You won't have time to read all of the questions first, but if you know there is a question on mood and another on irony, you can look for those aspects in the text and mark them as you read.

Be a reading Ninja! Think of each text on the exam as a noble, worthy opponent, but one that will not defeat you. Respect these literary opponents, recognize their strengths and special elements, but feel confident that you can read, understand, and respond to them. Never think you are too weak for any reading challenge!

ANNOTATING A TEXT

WHY ANNOTATE

When you read a difficult text, you're not usually reading for pleasure. Not even English teachers take Dostoevsky to the beach. Your goal is to understand the text and to read it as quickly as possible (especially on the AP Lit exam). Difficult texts are not easy to understand quickly, but annotating complex texts has several benefits:

- Marking key ideas (or those that seem at the moment to be important) engages your brain, improving active reading (as opposed to casual, leisure reading).

- Having marked a text, it is much easier and faster to go back and find evidence to prove a point or accurately choose an answer.

- Physically interacting with the text—putting pen to paper—is proven to improve your comprehension.

For example, if you are reading a poem and immediately recognize the dominant tone—mark that down. If the tone shifts in the last stanza—note that as well. If a question that follows the passage asks you to identify the tone, you'll most likely be able to answer it without rereading the text—all because you annotated!

HOW TO ANNOTATE

Critical to being able to effectively mark a text is knowing what to look for. Earlier in this text, you were given lists of literary elements and devices. If you have memorized how these literary tools function in general, it will be much easier for you to spot them at work in a particular passage.

In particular, annotating or marking a text means that as you read you underline key words, mark key phrases or ideas, and make margin notes. This process facilitates active and engaged reading. If you are making notes while you read and you are actively looking for what to mark, you will be less likely to drift off and to start thinking about something else. Again, the process of annotating trains you to recognize the most significant literary aspects of a poem or prose passage.

As you read, keep the elements of style and literature in mind. See Chapters 5 and 6.

PRACTICE ANNOTATING

Start practicing your annotating skills **now**, so you can train yourself. At first, practicing this skill may cause your reading speed to slow down. But, with time and practice, you'll be back to reading quickly and more deeply at the same time.

As you are learning this skill, practice annotating nearly everything you read. When you read, always have a pen or pencil in hand, even if you are reading a magazine. Once you've mastered the skills, you'll annotate only the texts you wish to study. Annotating is not something you would do for pleasure reading, unless your pleasure is to read and understand difficult books. If so, read with a pen in hand.

On the AP Lit exam, definitely use your annotating skills on the passages and poems in both the multiple-choice and free-response sections.

Once you've mastered your annotating skills, they'll serve you well for any analytical reading you do. You will have developed a skill that will help you read and study all kinds of texts in college and beyond, not just literary works.

Practice, practice, practice!

Leading up to the exam, you should be doing slower, more methodical annotations. However, closer to the exam, practice reading shorter passages, quickly annotating only the most important key ideas. In other words, when learning to ride this bicycle, you'll start out slow and deliberate, then later on ride as if in a race.

SUGGESTED SYMBOLS FOR ANNOTATING

Whether you use the suggested symbols below or create your own, it is important to keep it simple (use only a few symbols) and stay consistent.

(circle/oval symbol)	Circle unfamiliar words. You won't be allowed to use a dictionary on the AP Lit exam, but just circling unfamiliar words reminds you to try to understand them by using context clues. Prior to exam day, when you do have a dictionary available, look up the word if you cannot fully grasp its meaning from the context. Add these unfamiliar words to your list of words (see Chapter 9).
_____	Underline words in close proximity that share connotative or denotative associations.
!	An exclamation point in the margin near a group of lines indicates a key idea; pair with brackets around specific text
?	A question mark in the margin means "I don't understand." Noting your questions prompts you to answer them later.
text	Write brief notes in the margins to make your thinking visually accessible and easy to connect with when you take a second look at the text. Your notes can be about anything, but should include conclusions you've drawn about the text so far.
[ ]	Use brackets around phrases or chunks of text (or enclose in a rectangle) to mark significant literary elements, such as symbols, motifs (keep a count also), figurative language, etc. Label the element in the margin. Make corresponding notes about what these might mean. For example, don't simply mark that water is a symbol, but write a note about it being a symbol for purity that reinforces the innocence of the main character.

SAMPLE ANNOTATED TEXTS

The prose passage that follows is from Willa Cather's novel *My Antonia*. The poem that follows is John Donne's *The Broken Heart*. These samples are meant to give you an idea of what an annotated text looks like. As you study each one, you may find other literary elements that you would have marked or made note of. If so, it shows you are thinking critically. Good for you!!

Test Tip

Try writing an essay for each of the texts that follow using the insights in the annotations. Use this generic prompt to guide you: What is the narrator's/speaker's attitude toward the setting/situation?

Excerpt from *My Antonia* by Willa Cather

Jim Burden is narrating this passage.

I sat down in the middle of the garden, where snakes could scarcely approach unseen, and leaned my back against a warm yellow pumpkin. There were some ground-cherry bushes growing along the furrows, full of fruit. I turned back the papery triangular sheaths that protected the berries and ate a few. All about me giant grasshoppers, twice as big as any I had ever seen, were doing acrobatic feats among the dried vines. The gophers scurried up and down the ploughed ground. There in the sheltered draw-bottom the wind did not blow very hard, but I could hear it singing its humming tune up on the level, and I could see the tall grasses wave. The earth was warm under me, and warm as I crumbled it through my fingers. Queer little red bugs came out and moved in slow squadrons around me. Their backs were polished vermilion, with black spots. I kept as still as I could. Nothing happened. I did not expect anything to happen. I was something that lay under the sun and felt it, like the pumpkins, and I did not want to be anything more. I was entirely happy. Perhaps we feel like that when we die and become a part of something entire, whether it is sun and air, or goodness and knowledge. At any rate, that is happiness; to be dissolved into something complete and great. When it comes to one, it comes as naturally as sleep.

1st person narrator

Overall tone: contentment/contented tone.

Jim contemplates one of the big questions: What happens to us when we die?

* he's safe

he nestles into nature.

sustenance

entertaining place

Colors: warm reds & yellows & oranges reinforce warm feeling. Sun – yellow, too.

< tactile imagery ✯

He's one among them and he respects their movement an life. He won't scare the red bugs. He's also part of something bigger. Pantheism?

What is happiness but contentment?

What does it mean to be happy?

Not to fear – to welcome.

The contentment of the day extends to something more universal: the contentment of death, esp. if one dissolves "into some thing complete & great."

✯ Movement:
grasshoppers "doing acrobatic feats"
"gophers scurried"
"tall grasses wave"
Jim crumbles the earth through his fingers
bugs move in slow squadrons
Even the wind is active & singing
Our movement = our purpose
Action = Life We also move from life to death.

Life on earth is fully sustaining and we belong there as do pumpkins. But life beyond earth is also fully sustaining & where we belong.

Diction:
"Decay"-"devour"-
"plague"-"burn" } Suggest death, end of being.

Speaker is addressing a former love who broke his heart.

The Broken Heart

crazy
He is stark mad, who ever says, } Love doesn't last. Anyone who's really been in love knows this.
  That he hath been in love an hour,
Yet not that love so soon decays,
  But that it can ten in less space devour;
Who will believe me, if I swear
That I have had the plague a year? — love sickness — or been in love
  Who would not laugh at me, if I should say,
  I saw a flask of powder burn a day?

Love eats us alive as if we're nothing of value.

other griefs gave us something to feel.

Love is a grief, but a greedy one.

Ah, what a (trifle) is a heart, *meaningless*
  If once into love's hands it come!
All other griefs allow a part
  To other griefs, and ask themselves but some;
They come to us, but us Love draws,
He swallows us, and never chaws: ⟩ eats us whole — just gulps.
  By him, as by chain'd shot, whole ranks do die,
He is the tyrant pike, our hearts the fry.

Love personified — a voracious eater.

Love is the big fish ① and our hearts are the little fish ② that the big fish eats.

Metaphor — Love is compared to the pike —

proof (If 'twere not so, what did become
  Of my heart, when I first saw thee?)
I brought a heart into the room,
  But from the room, I carried none with me:
If it had gone to thee, I know
  Mine would have taught thine heart to show
More pity unto me: but Love, alas,
  At one first blow did shiver it as glass.

If my heart had gone to you — it would have taught you to have pity on me?

implies her heart was cruel.

Love at first sight.

When I first saw you I lost my heart.

shatter in shards like glass

Yet nothing can to nothing fall,
  Nor any place be empty quite,
Therefore I think my breast hath all
  Those pieces still, though they be not (unite;)
And now as broken glasses show
  A hundred lesser faces, so
My rags of heart can like, wish, and adore,
  But after one such love, can love no more.

—John Donne

one ②
mirrors (mini reflections)

But it is not logical that my breast is empty — so I must still have my heart although in "a million" pieces — all too small to reflect or love again.

torn/ shredded

(you)

Metaphor — Comparing broken heart to broken mirror.

Negative tone

his heart is ruined for love

Shattered glass cannot be mended.

After having loved you — my heart can no longer love. You broke my heart & ruined me for others.

Understanding Literary Analysis

". . . memorizing the name of a technique or being able to identify a technique is only the first step in analysis. The final step is to explain *how* a technique contributes to meaning," says the College Board in Student Performance Questions and Answers: AP English Literature and Composition Free-Response Questions. (2008)

In This Chapter

Overview

Key Concepts

Pitfalls and Biases

Typical Problems

Generating Your Analysis

CECT: A Formula to Remember

OVERVIEW

Analysis means to take apart and examine component parts of a whole in order to gain a greater understanding of the whole. The AP Lit exam gives you two opportunities to show your analysis skills. First, in the multiple-choice section, typically you'll read and answer questions for several prose passages and two poems. Implicit in choosing the correct answer is your analytical ability. Secondly, you will write three analytical essays in the free-response section.

Generally when we read a scholarly work and are expected to analyze and interpret our reading in an essay, we are given extensive time. We sometimes work with others through discussion to sort out our reactions. Such a written analysis goes through several drafts. However, the AP Lit exam puts your skills to a rigorous test by expecting lucid, insightful analysis in a very short time span—about three hours. The purpose of this chapter is to suggest ways for you to maximize your interpretative and analytical skills.

KEY CONCEPTS

Use this section to inform your basic understanding of literary analysis and its key concepts. Pair this section of the *Crash Course* with Chapter 15 for an expansive look at how to master AP English literary analysis essays.

LITERARY ANALYSIS

To write a literary analysis, you generally first read a text, develop an interpretation, and then gather the details from the text itself to defend your claim about some value of the text. See Chapter 14 for examples of Free-Response Prompts.

CLAIM

A claim is a statement of belief or an assertion of an idea, both of which require proof (evidence). All evidence for a literary analysis should come from the text.

Below is an example of a claim related to an analysis of contrasting characters from *The Scarlet Letter*:

> Hester Prynne's public admonition, while humiliating, eventually frees her from the weight of her sin, while Dimmesdale remains forever imprisoned by his guilt.

Were you to use the above claim in an essay analyzing contrasting characters in the novel, you would need to find evidence from the text to prove your assertion.

INACCURATE CLAIMS

Claims are based on interpretation, and interpretations differ because not everyone interprets a text in the same way. Since interpretations differ, your claims will also be different from those of others. But your claims should never be *inaccurate*. Inaccurate claims most often come about from a misreading of a text. Careful reading is your first step in literary analysis.

THESIS STATEMENT

A thesis statement is an essay's overarching claim (main claim) that establishes a writer's rhetorical purpose or line of reasoning. A thesis must be defensible. A good thesis statement may preview a line of reasoning.

A defensible thesis must meet the following criteria:

1. The thesis (or claim) is logical, and most readers of a text would agree to its validity, even if some would argue the opposite.

2. Sufficient evidence exists to prove the thesis (or claim).

EVIDENCE

Evidence refers to any element in the work of fiction, drama, or poetry that provides proof of a claim.

Evidence has several qualities:

1. Evidence must be apt, which means appropriate and relevant to the claim; apt also means the evidence is "enough" to prove the point. Some writers make excellent claims, but either fail to choose apt evidence or quit too soon in providing evidence.

2. Evidence must be sufficient. Some claims require more than one piece of evidence.

3. Evidence is not self-evident; it must be explained. See the "Commentary" section below.

4. According to the College Board, you are expected to use evidence strategically in order to "illustrate, clarify, exemplify, amplify, or qualify a point." See Chapter 8 for more about the verbs of rhetoric that will help you accomplish this goal.

LINE OF REASONING

A line of reasoning refers to the coherent progress of an argument throughout a literary analysis essay. Separate but related claims create the connecting points in a line of reasoning. In other words, a line of reasoning is a logical sequence of claims that, in cohesive combination, create a strong and valid argument.

BEYOND THE ORDINARY

What do highest-scoring essays have that medium-range essays don't? The College Board points to several factors that distinguish top essays. These factors are in addition to the other requirements of a solid literary analysis that show the writer's ability to make logical and relevant connections that add to an argument's impact.

1. **Creates a broader context.** Writers of top essays may explain the significance or relevance of an interpretation within a broader context. In other words, the writer brings the interpretation into a current setting. For example, a writer might discuss the injustice of Hester Prynne's public shaming in the context of the Me-Too movement.

2. **Includes alternative interpretations.** Top essays may discuss alternative interpretations, a similar tactic of a classic argument, where a writer recognizes and either concedes to or refutes an opposing viewpoint.

3. **Uses analogies.** Top essays may bring in analogies to help an audience understand the writer's interpretation, using a transition like "in other words," or "to put it in a contemporary setting," and then go on to link a similar situation.

Test Tip

If you're early in your AP English Lit exam prep, you can make it a standard goal to push your own essays "beyond the ordinary."

STRUCTURE

Every paragraph in a literary analysis essay should follow the same general structure:

1. Begin with your **claim**.

2. Follow with textual **evidence**.

3. Continue your argument through logical and rational **commentary**.

4. **Transition** to the next piece of evidence for the claim, if warranted. Otherwise, transition to the next paragraph.

You can use the mnemonic device "CECT" to help you remember these four steps. Be sure to follow them whenever you present evidence for a claim in an essay:

C: Claim

E: Evidence

C: Commentary

T: Transition

THE IMPORTANCE OF COMMENTARY

In order to make one's thinking clear or apparent, a writer needs to understand that evidence is not self-evident. You need to explain how or why the evidence proves your claim. This is called "Commentary." Then, moving on to the next claim, you need to use an effective transitional device.

RECURSIVE PROCESS

No doubt you were taught the basic writing process at some point: Ideate/Brainstorm, Draft, Revise, etc. On the AP exam, you have 120 minutes to write three Free-Response Essays. There's not a lot of time for the full-fledged writing process.

However, it is a fact that ideas tend to emerge from the act of writing itself. So, while you may have a solid grasp of your line of reasoning when you start to write, midway through your essay, a startling new claim—perhaps an even better claim—could emerge. It's perfectly okay to use the new idea in your writing, as long as it fits, works cohesively with what precedes it, and can be fully defended by evidence.

COHERENCE

Coherence is the quality of "fitting together." In grade school, you may have learned that a paragraph is a set of sentences that are related in idea. This is still true. But for AP English students, coherence is expected in the entire essay.

Create logical cohesion by using any of the following rhetorical methods:

- Transitions that link ideas and provide thought pathways for readers.

- Repetition devices that add emphasis.

- Parallel structures that reinforce key ideas.

AMBIGUITY

While ambiguity is an inherent quality of poetry due to imagery and figurative language, your own writing should not be ambiguous. If you've ever said, "That's not what I meant" in response to a critique of an essay you wrote, you might need to assess your use of unclear or ambiguous pronouns. In particular, beginning sentences with pronouns is a pitfall to avoid. Beginning sentences with pronouns is particularly detrimental if the antecedent for the pronoun (referent) lies in the preceding paragraph.

GRAMMAR AND MECHANICS

To be understood, you must have sufficient control over grammatical structures and mechanics, such as punctuation and yes, even spelling. Even a well-conceived thesis can be ruined if the writer is unable to compose direct, clear prose. Awkward or ambiguous wording will dilute your essay's otherwise excellent points. It can also result in a lowered test score for you.

See Chapter 15 for more about how to construct effective sentences and choose among various types of rhetorical structures to effectively communicate your ideas.

Test Tip

If you're aware of grammatical and mechanical errors in your own writing, it's best to address those weaknesses now. A writing tutor could help you identify and fix your problem areas.

ATTRIBUTION, CITATION, AND REFERENCES

You will not be using supplied resources for the Free-Response section of the English Lit exam in the same way you did (or will) on the AP English Language and Composition Exam. Nevertheless, you are expected to give credit where credit is due. If you make reference to an idea you read in an outside text, you need to cite the source of that idea. You can never take credit for the work or intellectual property of another, which is plagiarism. Use phrases like "according to" or "when [name of author] writes" to clearly indicate when you're using a borrowed idea. See more about this in Chapter 15.

You will also be citing lines and phrases from provided literary texts. Use line references when possible, and always put quotation marks around text citations you use in evidence, even single words. These practices are detailed in Chapter 15.

You will not be asked to use a particular attribution style guide, such as the *Chicago Manual of Style* or the *MLA Style Manual*. However, all the skills you've learned through your English and other classes for providing correct attribution should be evident in your writing for this exam.

PITFALLS AND BIASES

Use this section to challenge your own assumptions and biases. The list below summarizes problems AP readers encounter each year.

IT IS POSSIBLE

1. to misread a passage
2. to be arguing the wrong thing
3. to write about nothing
4. to choose the exact wrong word
5. to fail to answer the question

CONTROLLING YOUR BIASES

Misreading a passage comes more often from a limited or narrow world view than lack of reading skill. Therefore, learning about the factors that may influence your biases is valuable. Consider how the following points may apply to you. Simply acknowledging you have biases is the first step in minimizing their effect.

Perhaps the biggest obstacle for teens who are struggling to understand complex literary texts is their lack of life and world experience. There is only so much one can know at age 17 or 18.

We all have biases. They come from particular aspects of our lives that influence how we think. Biases are not wrong, but they can limit our ability to think with an open mind. This section is simply asking that you consider this important part of your thinking process and understand how biases can limit your ability to not only read and understand a poem or prose passage, but also limit your ability to write about it.

To avoid problems with biases, consider the following:

1. Watch for **undue sympathy,** or gut reactions, which tends to emerge from immature readers. For example, Wilbur's poem "The Death of a Toad" presents the last stages of a toad's life. Students who cannot get past the gross-out factor will remain stuck there and

will not be able to see the toad as an important actor in life's great pageant. Similarly, those who focus on the blood-stained sheet and feel only sympathy for the dead wolf in the passage from McCarthy's *The Crossing* might miss the fact that it is the young man we need to understand, not the wolf. To stay on track in a situation like this, focus on the prompt and the task it presents. Do not stray into emotional realms that are unrelated to your task.

2. Accept that you have **values and views** that might be particular and not universal. One's religious faith, ethnic heritage, political persuasion, or local social values, for example, sometimes limit one's ability to understand a text. It is not fair to expect a literary text to conform to your standards. The text is as it is. It is not wrong. It is not right. It is a text. To simplify: Do not judge the morality of a character or his situation unless that is the intent of the passage and indicated in the prompt.

3. Our **place in time** can be an impediment to our understanding. While it may be true that people of all times are more alike than different, society and culture do have an influence on our thinking. People who live in the age of technology have different concerns than those who lived prior to the industrial revolution. Applying the parameters of one's own time to all time is not wise. For example, never make uniformed blanket statements about the past, such as, "In the old days, people's lives were simpler." A good understanding of history will help you avoid such misstatements.

4. One limitation of immature readers is that they tend to see everything only through their **own experience**. If you've ever had a conversation with anyone who, instead of listening to what you have to say, jumps in with, "Oh, I know. That happened to me, too." and turns the focus to him- or herself, you have an idea of what can happen as you read, if you're not careful.

The experience or situation revealed in the poem or prose passage may indeed make you think about your own experience. And that is good because we don't really understand things we can't connect with. However, once you start formulating your thesis and working through your analysis, you must focus on the text. Your deep understanding of a passage or poem comes from the wisdom of your experience. However, the proof of your thesis must come from the text and not your experience.

TYPICAL PROBLEMS

This list of literary analysis problems comes from comments made by AP Lit readers about essays with lower scores. Four separate problem areas are presented in this section. Be sure to pay attention to the suggested solutions or strategies.

A: I READ AND UNDERSTOOD THE TEXT. WHY DID I GET A LOW SCORE?

Even if you have read a passage correctly and you've accurately grasped the main point of the text, you still may fail in your analysis if your essay exhibits any of the problems listed on the following pages:

Problem *The writer . . .*	*Solution/Strategy*
Fails to defend claims with textual evidence.	You cannot simply state claims without proving them. If your reader constantly needs proof, you have not done your job. If you say something is so, then you have to show how it is so by citing your evidence from the text.
Relies on only one or two claims and simply repeats those again and again.	Even if the points are excellent, repeating them again and again shows how thin your argument is. If you find yourself relying on one or two claims, go back to the text. What did you miss?
Provides too little analysis.	The writer doesn't go far enough. Some students are happy with a minimum effort. This attitude will not help you earn a high score. You should never just say, "good enough."
Is disorganized. His/her points are disconnected, illogically placed and inconsistently argued.	Disorganization seems to be the result of not having thought out your essay at the beginning. It is important to make a mini-outline in the margin of your page. While you may not follow it exactly, this outline will help you reconnect with points you wanted to make. A mini outline should also help you avoid digression. Find a good list of transitional words and phrases and learn to integrate them naturally into your writing. This will help you with organization. Don't be locked in to your mini-outline if you discover as you write a superior point, you need to make it.

Problem *The writer . . .*	*Solution/Strategy*
Has too many errors, such as blatant misspellings (author's name, title, characters etc.)	If a word is in the prompt or the passage, there is no excuse for misspelling it. Simply give a visual backward glance before proceeding. Misspelling easy words is not a good sign for AP-level students. Be careful. If you're using a difficult word, one you can use fluently when you speak, but you simply forget how to spell it, put a little "(sp.)" behind it, indicating that you forgot. It's one thing to misspell "ignominious" and another to write "metafor." You simply must know how to write complete and fluent sentences and punctuate them. See Chapter 15 for more help with this.
Does not explain why or show how his/her claim is true.	Stating a claim and giving evidence from the text is only part of your job as a writer. You also need to explain what you mean through coherent commentary. You need to show how or why what you say is true. Many times students think an idea is self-evident, so they leave it to explain itself. This is a poor strategy. Find sample essays that have been given high scores and analyze how those students develop their thinking with solid explanations.

Continued →

(Continued from previous page)

Problem *The writer . . .*	Solution/Strategy
Has too many claims.	If you have too many claims in support of your thesis, your analysis is most likely going to be superficial. It is best to settle on several significant aspects of the text, rather than point out every little thing. Your essay is not to be a frenzied show of how much you noticed, but instead, it should show your ability to distinguish between meaningless and truly arguable claims and between those that are, while true, somewhat flat in their relevance. If you have six claims you can argue, pick the best three or four. Depth, not breadth, is what is called for.

B: YOU'VE MISREAD PART OR ALL OF THE TEXT.

Problem *The writer . . .*	Solution/Strategy
Relies on paraphrase or summary.	Generally, this is what happens when you don't understand what you've read. If you don't really get the point of what you've read, but you know you've got to write something, you tend to simply restate the text or summarize it. If you do this, your score will be quite low. Summary is not analysis. To understand the reading, you need to look again for key points. (See Chapter 10 on reading and Chapter 12 on understanding themes.) Knowing what to look for will help you avoid misunderstanding.

Problem	
The writer . . .	*Solution/Strategy*
Has factual errors.	You misstate or misrepresent some aspect of the text. This does not mean you are misinterpreting—it means you are making faulty references, saying the text says one thing when it doesn't.
	The only way to fix this problem is through careful reading. You cannot replace careful reading with skimming. In the free-response section, in particular, you should not be skimming to find an answer to a question—you are reading to gain an in-depth understanding. See Chapter 10.
Makes an unnecessary observation.	You may be giving too much emphasis to a singular aspect of the text that may not be of value. Instead, base your claims on a broader understanding. In general, do not attribute too much meaning to one word or incident. On the other hand, one word can be critical, especially if it is isolated or repeated. Learn to see elements of a text in the context of the whole.
Has no real thesis, but instead gives a list of literary terms.	Many times the prompt suggests literary elements to consider in your analysis of the text, but these are means to an end. You must have some reason to mention them. There is no value in pointing out the evocative images in the second stanza if you don't intend to explain why they're important to the poem as a whole.

Continued →

(Continued from previous page)

Problem *The writer . . .*	*Solution/Strategy*
Fails to address the second poem (or passage).	The AP Lit exam will often provide two texts to consider for a compare/contrast exercise. Most often the texts to compare are poems. If you understand and write about only one and not the other, you will earn a low score because you are failing to meet the expectation of the prompt. In any compare/contrast exercise, look for the corresponding ideas, literary elements, and themes. A simple Venn diagram in the margin might help you organize your thoughts.
Presents contradictory claims.	There are two ways to think about this. One is that you lost track of what you were arguing and decided to go a different way, or, more likely, you weren't sure what the passage was about and you're struggling with meaning. I can't stress enough how important it is to do a careful reading, so you know what you want to argue. A mini-outline should help you avoid obvious contradictions in your own thinking.

Test Tip

If you have six claims you can argue in your essay, pick the best three or four. Depth, not breadth, is what is called for.

C: YOU MISREAD THE PROMPT

Problem	
The writer . . .	*Solution/Strategy*
Is completely off topic.	You perhaps charged too quickly out of the starting gate, with your eyes on the finish line (or the clock) instead of on your strategy for winning. You will not earn a high score if you're writing an essay different from the one you're expected to write. The prompt is carefully written to guide you. Use it. Read it several times. Underline the actual task. (See Chapter 14 for more help with this.)
Focuses on the wrong elements.	If the prompt lists specific literary elements to consider, pay attention to that list. The exam writers are telling you that these elements are at work in the text. If you go off on your own, you risk a limited or wrong analysis. On the other hand, they may be testing your ability to choose the most significant literary devices in a text from the list given. If you focus on the wrong choice, you risk a lower score. The key to choosing the right elements from a list is to take note of their prevalence or dominance. The more the literary element aids the writer in his or her purpose, the more you can write about it.
Has gone off topic and failed to connect with the main intent of the prompt.	According to the College Board, "prompts evolve from passages and are written to stimulate and open up discussion, not provide closure." However, once stimulated, your mind cannot journey somewhere unrelated to the prompt as that will be seen as a misreading.

Continued →

In choosing literary elements to consider for your essay, remember that in analyzing poetry, it will be rare that the rhyme scheme has any effect at all. While it is easy to determine a rhyme scheme, what will you say about its effect? It is not enough to identify literary elements. You must also show how they function in a literary work.

D: IMPRECISE USE OF LANGUAGE; IMPRECISE UNDERSTANDING OF LITERARY ELEMENTS

Problem *The writer . . .*	*Solution/Strategy*
Identifies techniques imprecisely.	For example, saying "flowy" instead of "fluent" shows a lack of scholarship. You must have a good knowledge of at least the basic literary terms (see Chapter 6). If you do not possess the terminology to say what you mean, you will struggle and your score will suffer.
Uses simplistic vocabulary.	One unstated aspect of your writing that AP readers note is your ability to use sophisticated vocabulary. Your essay should reflect both your understanding of a wide range of words and your skill to use them effectively. One should never stick in "fancy" words for the sake of doing so. Choosing the exact word for the job is part of being a good writer. If your own word choice is limited, your ability to express yourself may also be limited. (See Chapter 9 for more on vocabulary.)

GENERATING YOUR ANALYSIS

Step one: Read the prompt carefully.

Understand **exactly** what you are expected to do. Actually underline your specific task. This will give you a purpose for reading. If the prompt asks you, for example, to analyze the effect of an event on a character, then be looking exactly for that as you read. The prompt may or may not provide a short list of possible literary elements or devices that you can consider in analyzing how the writer achieves his or her purpose. When you read the passage or poem (step two), mark those devices and simultaneously be thinking how they help the author convey the effect of experience on the character. See Chapter 14 for an in depth look at prompts.

Test Tip

Consider everything given to you in a prompt as a hint or as information you need. Much like a Jeopardy question, there are often hints to the "answer" in the way the question is worded.

Step two: Read the poem or prose passage closely.

If your typical reading strategy is to skim, you are putting yourself in analytical peril. In other words, when you are given a passage to analyze, you are expected to cite the text in evidence, which will be difficult if you read superficially. The essay section counts for 55% of your cumulative score, so it seems logical that you'd want to give the three essays your best effort.

To reiterate, don't think that skimming the reading will save you time. In the long run, you'll be at a huge disadvantage. Instead, use the tips in Chapter 10 on engaged and active reading to help you read both quickly and deeply. As you read, annotate the text, marking significant aspects of the text as they relate to the task laid out in the prompt.

Step three: Create a **mini-outline**.

In the margin of your test page (the one with the prompt on it), draft a quick thesis and outline several main claims in support of your thesis. Use symbols to connect those prompts to corresponding evidence in the text. For example, give claim #1 a star and put stars by everything in the text that relates. You may not use it all in your essay, but identifying it is an important step in creating a well-organized and detailed analysis.

Step four: Write your essay.

Begin writing your essay. Be sure to minimize the effect of biases, be mindful of your word choices, and be sure your points are well argued. (See Chapter 15 for more on essay writing.) Be sure to use the outline you created to keep you focused. However, if you discover something you didn't see before as you write, and you are sure that the new discovery is important, pay attention to it. Do not be too constrained by your initial outline. However, if your first insight is spot on, then by all means, stick to your outline as a means to stay on point.

CECT: A FORMULA TO REMEMBER

Remember "CECT" and you'll remember the main elements of a good argumentative essay:

C State a **CLAIM**

E Provide **EVIDENCE** from the text

C Provide **COMMENTARY** that explains your thinking

T Provide a smooth, logical **TRANSITION** to the next idea.

See more about CECT in Chapter 15.

As you are writing, if you discover something you didn't see before, and you are sure that the new discovery is important, pay attention to it. Do not be too constrained by your initial outline.

So What? Understanding Literary Themes

OVERVIEW

Each summer, my AP students read Jostein Gaarder's novel of the history of Western philosophy, *Sophie's World*. They read it so we could begin our year of literary study with a better understanding of the key questions that have concerned human beings for all of recorded history—questions like "Who am I?," "Is there life after death?," and my personal favorite, "How ought we to live?" The questions that drive philosophers are almost always the same questions that drive literary writers. Truly great works of literature are always about something—there is always a point. And the point, the "so what" in a significant work of literature is a theme that is universal and timeless. Such a theme is largely true for all people of all times and in all places.

WHAT IS "SO WHAT?"

To write a good essay for the AP Lit exam, you must discover the thematic truth in the poem or prose text you are given. Not everyone will see the same truth in a work, but the texts chosen for each exam do have important ideas in them. You will always be asked to "zoom in" on an important idea, the thing I call the "So What." In other words, when I read a poem, I ask "So what?" What is it about this poem that really matters? What is the point that the writer is trying to make?

Once you discover that underlying idea, then you'll analyze **the ways the poet or author reveals that theme** to readers through a variety of literary elements. It will never be enough to simply recognize figurative language or imagery. If that is all you do, the reader of your essay may also ask, "So what?"

Therefore, "So What" can be viewed in two ways:

1. the universal theme of a poem or prose text, or

2. your insight into that theme as revealed through your careful analysis of literary elements.

Understanding of a universal theme or truth must drive your essay. Without it, you are writing about nothing. Without it, your reader will ask, "So what?"

SO WHAT? A VISUAL GUIDE*

SO WHAT IS THE WHY.

So What is the true meaning of a story.

...there is always a point.

So What is what makes a piece of literature matter. It is what makes it full, not flat.

The author is saying something that is universally true.

There is universal meaning in the passage, something that relates to real life.

The writer refers to both the writer of the literary passage and the student writer who is struggling to make meaning of the text.

There is no reason for an essay without a So What.

The universal truth the writer (student) will explain.

The So What is the unifying idea that keeps the writer (student) on track. Without it, you can forget why you're writing in the first place.

The So What of an essay is the point the writer is trying to make.

Without it, [a student's essay] will prompt the reader to say, "so what. What is the significance of this essay."

The So What statement is located in the [student's] introduction, but it should also be apparent throughout the essay. It should drive the essay.

It is a universal truth that everyone can learn from or relate to.

It is the profound message that the author is trying to get the reader to understand--often a moral or a life lesson.

*This visual guide was created with help from the author's 2010 AP English Literature class.

▌ COMMON LITERARY THEMES

THEMATIC STATEMENTS:

- All life is connected.
- Each life, no matter how small, matters.
- Life is too brief.
- Youth (innocence) and beauty don't last.
- We don't appreciate what we have until it's gone.
- Pride can blind us to the truth.
- Small acts of kindness and/or generosity can have a tremendous effect.
- Courage can reward those who push themselves.
- Sometimes we learn too late what we need to know.
- Social status, beauty, wealth, etc., do not matter.
- We learn through trial, hardship, or pain those lessons most valuable.
- The individual is sometimes in conflict with society.
- Individuals are often alienated and alone.
- Self-determination is a fierce inner force, but is often thwarted or delayed by outside forces.
- Fantasy is sometimes more real than everyday reality.
- Mortality (death) is inevitable.
- Human beings are sometimes too weak (or too blind) to do what is right.
- We often want what others have or we often want what we cannot have.
- Fear, jealousy, and greed are destructive emotions.

- We sometimes hurt those we love.

- People (of all cultures and of all times) are more alike than they are different.

- Nature does not care about people.

- Each of us is alone (often feeling small or frightened) in the world.

- Even good people can do hurtful or cruel things.

THEMATIC QUESTIONS:

- What is truth?

- What is beauty?

- What is real?

- What is justice?

- What is honor?

- What is love?

- What does it mean to live a good life?

- What does it mean to be a hero?

- What does it mean to have courage?

Test Tip

Make a card listing your ten favorite literary themes and carry it with you. Look at it often. These themes can serve as the lens through which you view the world. You will start to hear these themes in songs, see them in movies, and even recognize them on TV shows. More importantly, you will be better able to recognize them in the literature you read. The result of "practicing" themes is that when you read complex passages and poems on the AP Lit exam, you will be able to recognize the "so what" quickly.

Point of View:
From Whose Perspective?

"You never really understand a person until you consider things from his point of view."

—Atticus Finch in Harper Lee's *To Kill a Mockingbird*

OVERVIEW

There are two main ways to consider point of view: the point of view in the passage that you are to identify and your own point of view as you consider the passage and what it means. This chapter will help you to realize the importance of both.

YOUR OWN POINT OF VIEW

An inherent disadvantage to youth is that it comes with a limited world view. Most high school students have limited life experience. We cannot blame them for this, but as experience affects one's ability to conceive of complex literary themes, it is a matter worth addressing here. In addition, each of us, despite our age, can work to broaden our experience so we can have an even fuller world view.

In addition to your age, your point of view is influenced by your

- culture: ethnicity, religion, etc.

- environment: urban, rural, specific region of the country

- family values

- economic status

- actual life experiences: travel, personal interactions with people who are different from you, even having been in love

These influences cause us to have particular biases. Everyone has biases. It is important for us to recognize that fact and understand that our point of view and our biases affect how we read. To be good critical readers, we must control and limit the effect of our biases.

ROLE OF REAL-LIFE EXPERIENCES

One of the best ways to understand literature and its themes is to read. But sometimes we need to have experiences that help us understand what we read. To do this, consider expanding your knowledge of the world in the following ways:

- Engage in conversations with people from different cultures
- Talk to older adults about their life experiences
- Add variety to your media preferences:
    - read a variety of books (see Chapter 4)
    - listen to different types of music
    - watch foreign films, with subtitles
    - read national and international newspapers
    - watch The History Channel
    - download lectures and philosophy podcasts and listen to them

BECOME AN EMPATHETIC READER

Empathy is *the ability to put ourselves in someone else's place, to see things as he or she sees them.* As readers, we must be empathetic if we are to truly understand the characters in the books we read. To do this, it means you have to actually put yourself in the place of the speaker, the narrator, or the character.

When you read, visualize yourself in the text. Make a "mind movie" in which you walk through the setting, follow the characters, listen to them speak, and observe their actions. Even more importantly, allow yourself to feel what the character feels. This is empathy.

Many questions on the AP Lit exam ask you to determine the attitude or the reaction of a character or speaker to an event. If you become an empathetic reader, this task will be much easier for you.

The more you practice empathetic reading, the more you will develop a kind of "double vision," in which you'll view the text from both within and without. You will become a reader who sees the parts of the text as they relate to the whole.

In your double vision, you'll learn to appreciate how the writer conveys enduring and universal ideas through the perspective of a character, narrator, or speaker.

THE IMPORTANCE OF IRONY AND TONE

Many AP readers say that students have difficulty recognizing irony in passages on the exam. Questions about irony are prevalent in the multiple-choice section. Recognizing irony is an aspect of seeing clearly. If something is not what it seems, perhaps there is something ironic. But beyond simply recognizing an instance of irony, you will need to determine the effect irony has in the text as a whole.

Dramatic irony is a powerful tool authors employ to reveal thematic insight. Whenever you know something a character or speaker does not know or is not aware of, you should make note of the discrepancy in the margin of the text. As you follow your character around in your "mind movie," pay attention to moments when you feel smarter or more aware than he is. What do these moments show you?

A character's speech is not always meant to be taken literally. Watch for **verbal irony** *when what a character says is different from what she really means.* The voice may even be sarcastic. Look for the underlying truth and how that truth functions in the text.

Lastly, watch for evidence of **situational irony**. This can be *a discrepancy in the setting or situation that is not what you expect.* For example, you'd not expect a very wealthy widow to be eating cat food. What might such a detail mean?

TONE

Tone is *the writer's attitude toward the writing itself; toward the subject; toward the people, places, time and events in the passage and/or toward the audience.* Tone is an important tool in understanding what the writer is saying. The writer's tone or attitude may be serious, humorous, sarcastic, ironic, pessimistic, critical, objective, or playful. Indeed, the author's feelings may be any of the attitudes and feelings that human beings experience. The author will create a specific tone that reinforces how the narrator, speaker, or character feels about someone or something. The author's style reveals these attitudes to the reader. When you are asked to determine the speaker's reaction to an event, look for the underlying emotions in any passage.

Test Tip

When you select texts to read prior to your exam, look for a variety of points of view. For example, don't read only first or third person narrators. Mix things up.

REVIEWING MAIN POINTS OF VIEW

- **First person:** the narrator tells his/her own story using first-person pronouns. This point of view is limited by what the narrator can know, see, or understand. First-person narrators cannot always be trusted to assess the situation honestly. They may be blind to their own faults, etc.

- **Second person:** the narrator uses second-person pronouns to make immediate connections with readers (a very rare point of view in fiction).

- **Third-person limited:** a third-person narrator tells the story (generally the main character's story, but sometimes tells the story from a peripheral character's viewpoint) using third person pronouns. A third-person limited narrator is similar to a first-person narrator in that he can only see and know what his character can see and know.

- **Third-person omniscient:** this third-person narrator is god-like, seeing and knowing all without constraints of time or space, seeing even beyond earthly existence. Third-person narrators often digress into contemplative or philosophical forays. Third person omniscient narrators will sometimes voice the viewpoint of the author.

- **Objective:** an objective narrator tells a story like a video recorder would, simply revealing the sights and sounds it perceives (though not, of course, as strictly as that). Recognize an objective narrator by that person's lack of emotion or personal interest in the subject.

Test Tip

Remember, you can't always trust a first person narrator. Be a careful and critical reader, and you'll know what she does not know.

SHIFTS IN POINT OF VIEW

A shift in point of view is something to pay close attention to. It is often a critical marker in understanding meaning or theme. Use the following list of questions as your guide and make notes in your annotations.

1. Identify the shift. Where does it occur? From whose point of view to whose?

2. Why does the shift occur? What can the author accomplish with this new narrative point of view?

3. What changes are evident in narrative style, narrative voice, even syntax and diction?

4. What can you see that you did not see before? Something new? Something different? Something opposite?

5. What limitation exists?

6. What does this new "viewer" know that the previous one did not? Or vice versa.

7. What is the overall effect of the shift?

Pull all of your observations together to create a defensible claim for an essay.

CONTROLLING POINT OF VIEW IN YOUR OWN ESSAY

LITERARY PRESENT TENSE

Characters live in the present time in the novel. To write about them, we use what is called the *literary present tense*. Atticus *is* a great father to Scout and Jem. Odysseus *plugs* his ears with wax so he won't *hear* the Siren's song. Be cautious when you weave in text citations that are primarily in the past tense. You need to create sentences that are clear and grammatically correct. Mixing verb tenses can be very confusing. If you must change the tense in a quoted passage, use [brackets] around the parts you change.

AUTHORITATIVE THIRD PERSON

A literary analysis essay, like the ones you write for the AP Lit exam, are best written in third person, which gives you an authoritative voice. Since you are writing from your own viewpoint, it is a natural tendency to want to qualify your opinions by adding phrases such as "I think," "I feel," and "In my opinion." It is a much stronger practice to avoid such qualifiers and write strong, confident claims as if they are fact. It will be your task to defend your claims well so that your reader accepts your opinions, but don't intentionally limit them with qualifying phrases. Think of how you respond to the examples below. Which one of each pair seems stronger, more like a fact?

Qualified Claim	Authoritative Claim
In my opinion, Scout learns that being a lady is about honor and integrity, not dresses.	Scout learns that being a lady is about honor and integrity, not dresses.
When Juliet warns Romeo to "swear not by the moon, the inconstant moon/That monthly changes in her circled orb" I think she means that	When Juliet warns Romeo to "swear not by the moon, the inconstant moon/That monthly changes in her circled orb" she means that . . . .

UNIVERSAL FIRST PERSON

Generally, we use third person in literary analysis essays. However, there are times when first person seems perfectly correct for the point we want to make. We use universal first person when we include ourselves in all the masses who understand universal truths or themes. We'll use "we" instead of "I" to show our alliance in a common understanding or purpose. It may be appropriate to use the universal first-person point of view, especially in your essay's conclusion if you extend your theme as something we all know or should know.

PART IV:

ESSAY INSIGHTS

Free-Response Questions:
Analysis of Prompts

OVERVIEW

This chapter summarizes the types of prompts that have
appeared on previous AP Lit exams. Free-response prompts tend to
have some consistent qualities. Knowing these qualities can help
you to be prepared for your own exam day.

THREE TYPES OF FREE-RESPONSE QUESTIONS

1. A prose passage is provided (generally fiction, but
   sometimes drama or nonfiction) for you to analyze.

2. A poem (or two for comparison) is provided for you
   to read and analyze.

3. A general question is provided along with a list of possible works that fit the prompt. It is up to you to choose the work that is the best fit for the question. You <u>must</u> choose a work you know well. It <u>must</u> be a work of literary merit (see Chapter 4).

PROMPTS, IN GENERAL

An essay prompt does several things:

1. Asks you to carefully read (or recall) a specific text.

2. Gives you a content task to accomplish (see examples later in this chapter).

3. Gives you a hint about the main theme of a passage or poem or openly states a theme or point of view to consider for the open-ended question on the AP exam.

4. May, or may not, give you a brief list of literary elements to consider in your argument.

5. Directly tells you to write a well-organized essay.

For example, let's analyze a prose prompt from a released exam from the novel *The White Heron*. See Chapter 15 for a sample essay for this prompt.

Prompt	Analysis of the Prompt
"Read the following passage carefully. Then write an essay **showing how the author dramatizes the young heroine's adventure**. Consider such literary elements as diction, imagery, narrative pace, and point of view."	**Content task:** [show] how the author dramatizes the young heroine's adventure.
	Literary elements to consider are given: diction, imagery, narrative pace, and point of view.
	Notes:
	As you read the passage, you need to understand the heroine's adventure. What is it? Why is it an adventure? How is it dramatic, or dramatized?
	The writers of this prompt suggest that you also consider the author's choice of words, imagery, narrative pace, and point of view.
	These are more than suggestions—they are strong hints. Don't ignore them!
	In fact, this text includes an interesting shift in point of view that would be a mistake to ignore. You will need to determine the effect of that shift.
	Also, it's not enough to pick out strong images or great word choices. You must show how these elements help the author dramatize the young heroine's adventure.

Test Tip

It is critically important for you to know exactly what a prompt is asking for and respond appropriately. You will earn a very low score if you fail to do what the prompt asks you to do.

Find more prompts from released exams online at AP Central (*https://apcentral.collegeboard.org*). This is a valuable College Board website to help you study.

PROSE PASSAGE PROMPTS

The information that follows comes from an analysis of prose prompts from released exams.

Content Task	Key Elements
Analyze the style and tone of the passage, explaining how they help to express the author's attitude.	style/tone author's attitude
Discuss the ways the author differentiates between the writing of (author one) and that of (author two).	compare two texts
Analyze the narrative techniques and other resources of language the author uses to characterize a mother and the mother's attitude toward her daughter.	characterization characters' attitudes
Define the author's view and analyze how he conveys it.	characterization
Show how the author dramatizes a young heroine's adventure.	characterization
Analyze how the author uses literary techniques to characterize _____.	characterization
Analyze how the narrator reveals the character of _____.	characterization
Analyze how changes in perspective and style reflect the narrator's complex attitude toward the past.	narrator's attitude

Content Task	Key Elements
Write an essay in which you characterize the narrator's attitude toward _____ and analyze the literary techniques used to convey this attitude.	narrator's attitude characterization
Show how the author's techniques convey the impact of the experience on the main character.	characterization
Analyze how the language of the passage characterizes the diarist and his society and how the characterization serves _____ satiric purpose.	characterization compare/contrast analysis of satire
Analyze the techniques that the author uses to characterize _____ and _____.	characterization compare/contrast
Analyze how the author produces a comic effect.	narrative effect, comedy
Analyze how the author's use of language generates a vivid impression of _____ as a character.	characterization general use of language
Explain how the author uses narrative voice and characterization to provide a social commentary.	social commentary characterization narrative voice
Analyze the author's depiction of the three characters and the relationships among them.	characterization compare/contrast
Analyze how the author uses elements such as point of view, selection of detail, dialogue, and characterization to make a social commentary.	elements of literature social commentary

Continued ➞

Content Task	Key Elements
Show how the author uses literary devices to achieve her purpose.	The task is vague, perhaps on purpose. In this case, you'd be expected to determine the author's purpose first.
Discuss how the characterization in the passage reflects the narrator's attitude toward _____.	characterization narrator's attitude
Analyze how the playwright reveals the values of the characters and the nature of their society.	point of view of characters characterization of society
Discuss how the narrator's style reveals his attitudes toward the people he describes.	narrator's attitude characterization
Analyze how the author uses techniques to characterize the relationship between a young man and his father.	characterization
Analyze how the author uses literary devices to characterize _____ experience.	characterization point of view of character
Analyze how the author establishes _____ relationship to the urban setting.	characterization point of view of character analysis of elements of literature: setting
Analyze the literary techniques the author uses to describe _____ and to characterize the people who live there.	analysis of elements of literature: setting

POETRY PROMPTS

The information that follows comes from an analysis of poetry prompts from released exams. About one-third of the free-response prompts for poetry ask you to compare elements in two poems.

Content Task	Key Elements
Show how the use of language reveals the speaker's attitude toward _____.	speaker's attitude
Trace the speaker's changing responses to his experience and explain how they are conveyed by the poem's diction, imagery, and tone.	speaker's response/attitude changes/shifts
Discuss how such elements as language, imagery, structure, and point of view convey meaning.	vague allusion to theme: would need to determine meaning on your own
Considering such elements as speaker, diction, imagery, form, and tone, write a well-organized essay in which you contrast the speakers' views of _____.	compare/contrast speakers' point of view
Analyze how the speaker uses the imagery of the poem to reveal his attitude toward _____.	speaker's attitude
Discuss how the poem's controlling metaphor expresses the complex attitude of the speaker.	speaker's attitude
Explain how formal elements such as structure, syntax, diction, and imagery reveal the speaker's response to _____.	speaker's response (point of view)
Analyze how the poem reveals the speaker's complex conception of _____.	speaker's point of view

Continued →

(Continued from previous page)

Content Task	Key Elements
Explain how the poet conveys not just a literal description of _____ but a deeper understanding of the whole experience.	poet's point of view
Compare the portrayals of the _____.	compare/contrast
Analyze how the author uses elements such as allusion, figurative language, and tone to convey the speaker's complex response to his dismissal from court.	speaker's point of view
Analyze how the poet employs literary devices in adapting the Greek myth to a contemporary setting.	compare/contrast
Analyze how the poet uses language to portray the scene and convey mood and meaning.	analysis of setting, mood
Discuss how the poet uses literary techniques to reveal the speaker's attitude toward _____ and _____.	speaker's attitude
Compare and contrast two poems, analyzing the significance of _____ in each of the poems.	compare/contrast analysis of setting
Analyze the techniques the poet uses to develop the relationship between the speaker and the setting.	speaker's point of view analysis of setting

Test Tip

Start reading different kinds of poems. For each one, determine what the speaker's attitude is and how you know it. Knowing the speaker's attitude about someone or something is one of the main tasks given in poetry prompts.

OPEN-ENDED PROMPTS

The information that follows comes from an analysis of prompts for question three from released exams. An open-ended question encourages a full, meaningful answer in which you rely on your own knowledge or feelings.

Nearly all of these prompts warn you to <u>avoid</u> plot summary. They also expect you to choose an appropriate work of literary merit. "Appropriate" means that you can defend your thesis by references to that work.

Main Thematic Focus	Main Literary Focus
Show how a character's alienation reveals the surrounding society's assumptions and moral values.	character's conflict
Show how a character is caught between colliding cultures — national, regional, ethnic, religious, institutional.	character's conflict
Analyze how tension between outward conformity and inward questioning contributes to the meaning of a work.	analysis of elements of literature: theme
Show how a specific death scene helps to illuminate the meaning of a work.	analysis of elements of literature: theme
Choose a character whose private passion conflicts with his or her responsibilities. In your essay show the nature of the conflict, its effects upon the character, and its significance to the work.	character's conflict
Show the author's purpose for including a struggle for dominance.	author's style/technique

Continued →

(Continued from previous page)

Main Thematic Focus	Main Literary Focus
Choose an important character who is a villain. Then analyze the nature of the character's villainy and show how it enhances meaning in the work.	analysis of elements of literature: character
Explain how a scene or scenes of violence contribute to the meaning of the complete work.	analysis of elements of literature: theme
Analyze the sources of a conflict between a parent and a son or daughter and explain how the conflict contributes to the meaning of the work.	character's conflict
Show how the presentation of a character considered evil or immoral creates more sympathy in us than would normally be expected.	analysis of elements of literature: character
Describe how an author presents mental or psychological events, such as awakenings or discoveries, or a sense of excitement, suspense, or climax.	author's style/technique
Show how the author's manipulation of distinct elements of time contributes to the effectiveness of the work as a whole.	author's style/technique
Show how a morally ambiguous character plays a pivotal role in a work and how his or her moral ambiguity is significant to the work as a whole.	analysis of elements of literature: character
Select a tragic figure who functions as an instrument of suffering in others and explain how the suffering contributes to the tragic vision of the work as a whole.	analysis of elements of literature: character

Continued ➞

(Continued from previous page)

Main Thematic Focus	Main Literary Focus
Choose a scene or character that creates thoughtful laughter in the reader and show why this laughter is thoughtful and how it contributes to the meaning of the work.	analysis of elements of literature: setting or character
Show how the opening scene of a play or the first chapter of a novel introduces some of the major themes of the work.	analysis of elements of literature: structure
Show how a wedding, funeral, party, or other social occasion reveals the values of the characters and the society in which they live and discuss the contribution the scene makes to the work.	analysis of elements of literature: setting/scene
Show how a character who appears briefly, or does not appear at all, is a significant presence in a work, explaining how he or she functions in the work.	analysis of elements of literature: character
Many stories are about an individual who opposes the will of the majority. Select a character who is in opposition to his or her society and discuss the moral and ethical implications for both the individual and the society.	character's conflict
Identify and explain an allusion that predominates a work and analyze how it enhances the meaning.	author's style/technique

Continued →

(Continued from previous page)

Main Thematic Focus	Main Literary Focus
Show how the character's relationship to the past contributes to the meaning of the work.	character's conflict
Choose a minor character who serves as a foil to a main character and analyze how the relationship between the foil character and the major character illuminates the meaning of the work.	analysis of elements of literature: character
Analyze how a symbol functions in a work and what it reveals about the characters or themes of the work as a whole.	analysis of elements of literature: symbol

Test Tip

Know the basic elements of character: appearance, speech, thoughts, actions, and what others think of him or her. Of these, speech and action sometimes conflict, just as with real people. It is in these discrepancies that truth emerges.

Essay Basics

"Persuasion is achieved by the speaker's personal character when the speech is so spoken as to make us think him credible."

—Aristotle in *Rhetoric*

OVERVIEW

You need not compose the most brilliant essays you've ever written to do well on the AP Lit exam. But you must show that you understand the texts, that you can formulate logical, defensible arguments, and that you can write well-organized and insightful essays. Nonetheless, your essays for the exam will be considered drafts, and AP readers are instructed to award points for what students do well. This chapter sets out what you need to know to write the best essays possible in the time allotted. Use this chapter in conjunction with a thorough understanding of Chapter 11.

ABOUT THE ESSAYS

You will be writing three essays in two hours, which gives you approximately 40 minutes for each essay. In this 40 minutes you must read the text, understand it, formulate your thesis, and write a well-developed and well-organized literary analysis essay.

Chapter 14 contains an analysis of essay prompts from released exams. The list describes the kinds of questions that typically guide the AP Lit essays. There is always an essay on a poem (or a comparison of two poems), a prose passage (fiction or nonfiction essay), and finally an open-ended question for which you must supply an appropriate text.

TYPICAL PROBLEMS

If you were to ask an AP reader to list some typical mistakes students make in writing their essays, he or she would most likely mention the following:

- no discernible thesis (therefore, no controlling idea)
- a failure to analyze (the writer summarized or paraphrased instead)
- a failure to move from "what" to "how" and "why"

- a failure to support generalizations or claims with evidence from the text

- only poorly developed ideas, with perhaps one or two ideas repeated over and over

- an inability to integrate and embed quotations from the text in complete sentences

- a wordy introduction that was mostly a restatement of the prompt

- a "boring" conclusion that simply restated the thesis or prompt

- some loosely constructed paragraphs that were not unified

- a reliance on the five-paragraph essay, with no real analysis. (Organization without content is not an essay.)

- imprecise use of language. (Never use big words to impress—use the exact word for your purpose.)

GENERAL QUALITIES OF A GOOD ESSAY

- A relatively short essay with a defensible thesis and a few insightful claims supported with textual evidence is better than a longer essay that is about nothing. (If you don't understand the prompt or the text, your essay will be about nothing.)

- An essay is not a list of separate ideas clumped together.

- An essay is not a summary of the text—it is an argument that you control. (A generalization without support is not an argument.)

- A thesis needs to respond accurately to the task given in the prompt.

- A good essay is well organized, even if it is a draft. It should have discernible parts: introduction, body, and conclusion.

ELEMENTS OF A GOOD INTRODUCTION

- The task given in the prompt must be acknowledged in your introduction.

- The writer's name and the title of the work must be given. (Correct spelling is essential.)

- You cannot take time for windy prose meant to engage the reader. The introduction needs to be precise allowing you to jump into your argument.

- Include a thesis that reveals your insightful understanding of the key ideas in the text.

MORE ON THESIS STATEMENTS

A thesis statement is *the sentence where you state your purpose* or what you intend to prove in your essay. If you don't have something to argue, there is no thesis. While reading, you must come to some conclusion or interpretation about the text, something you believe about the text that you can defend and support. Your thesis will come from that. An effective thesis statement will serve as your guide.

Test Tip

If you need a formula for constructing a solid thesis sentence, try this one: Thesis = statement acknowledging task + statement showing your insightful recognition of theme (your "so what") or clear statement of your interpretation.

Two sentences may be needed to accomplish your thesis presentation. That is perfectly acceptable. However, aim for fewer rather than more words to say what you need to say.

DEVELOPING THE BODY OF THE ESSAY

The body of your essay is *where you argue your thesis*. You will need to make several points or claims that prove your thesis. A good *formula* for developing the ideas in your argument is the "CECT" formula:

> 1) State a **Claim**. (This may be your topic sentence in a paragraph.)
>
> 2) Defend the claim with **Evidence** from the text.
>
> 3) Explain your reasoning through careful **Commentary**, especially showing how or why.
>
> 4) **Transition** to more evidence, commentary, to the next claim, or to the next paragraph.

Test Tip

As you write practice essays, use a different highlighter for each "CECT" element to be sure you are indeed writing an analysis and not a summary.

MORE ON COMMENTARY, EXPLAINING YOUR REASONING

Sometimes you will think that your ideas are clearly stated when they're actually only implicit (implied). You need to make your ideas explicit, meaning *you need to show exactly how and/or why what you say is so*. Make connections. Make your ideas transparent. One of the biggest problems in student essays is the existence of too many implied ideas.

If you (or your reader) ask the following questions about your essay, you have not fully explained what you mean:

- Why?

- What is important or significant about this idea?

- What does this have to do with the claim?

STRUCTURING THE ESSAY

You should let your essay develop organically from what you know. There is no set number of paragraphs expected for your AP essays, but avoid using the five-paragraph formula. It can be too constrictive, and it may have you thinking more about the formula than your ideas. For example, if you limit yourself to three body paragraphs, you may end up eliminating a fourth, excellent point, or worse, you will try to squeeze it in a paragraph where it does not logically belong. Your paragraphs need not be the same length either. If you make your point in three sentences and want to move on to the next paragraph, then do so. The next point you make may need seven sentences. Let your argument determine the structure of your essay.

WRITING A CONCLUSION THAT INSPIRES: QUALITIES OF A GOOD CONCLUSION

Avoid generic summary conclusions that simply restate the thesis. They're boring and rob you of the opportunity to go beyond your analysis of a text to relate your insight. While your conclusion should not be overly personal, your particular insight does come from you and sometimes the conclusion is where your voice is most strong. Still, remember to stay focused on the text.

SOME CONCLUSION TIPS:

- Never introduce a new idea (a new claim) in the conclusion.

- Generally, do not cite the text in the conclusion.

- Remind the readers of the most important concepts of your essay.

- A good conclusion makes the essay feel finished.

- Avoid cliché phrases like "in conclusion," "to sum up," or the like. However, you still need to make a smooth transition to the end of the essay.

"BUT, WHAT IF I RUN OUT OF TIME?"

It is possible that you will not have time to write a conclusion. Of course it is best if you can end with something, even a sentence or two, but in the event that the proctor is standing over you with his hand out, your essay will have to leave you without its ending. Do not fret. The introduction and the body are the most crucial parts and should show your insightful analysis. It is possible to score well without a true conclusion.

Test Tip

The best preparation for writing a complete AP Lit essay in 40 minutes is to practice, practice, practice! It takes a lot of effort, but your diligence will be rewarded.

INTEGRATING OR EMBEDDING TEXTUAL EVIDENCE

Weaving textual evidence into an essay is a skill that you can practice and learn to do well. You should study good models. Reading a newspaper can help you. Journalists are experts at integrating quotations into their text. They must attribute quotations to their sources as well. Even though they're not quoting literary texts, they do follow similar guidelines for embedding their quotations. You can also look at student models (the top-scoring essays) at the AP Central website.

Learn these rules for integrating textual evidence:

- You need to supply context for a full or partial quotation. This means to set it up somehow, or transition into the quotation with your claim.

- As a general rule, don't start a sentence with a quotation.

- Use quotation marks around anything you take from the text, even isolated words.

- When you weave in the cited text, you must end up with a grammatically correct sentence. If you have to change tense or wording, use [brackets] around the parts you change.

- Use strong verbs when you refer to the writer (poet, speaker, etc.). Notice the verbs in the model phrases below.

- Use slashes (/) to separate lines of poetry from one another.

Some model phrases to consider:

- The writer (poet) or speaker argues, claims that, suggests, etc._____. His description of "_____."

- "_____" reads quickly, even frantically. This narrative pace suggests that _____.

- When _____(author) writes that _____, she shows how "_____."

- The imagery in stanza four contrasts with stanza one. "_____" suggests something, while "_____" is clearly meant to _____.

- _____(Character's name) feels trapped by her situation. She "_____."

- "_____," "_____," and "_____" are words commonly heard in church, which gives the passage _____ .

When you read student essay samples from the AP Central website, look specifically at how the writers of top-scoring essays incorporate evidence from the text to defend their claims.

QUOTING THE TEXT: TIPS AND STRATEGIES

- Use partial quotations. You will seldom need to quote an entire sentence from a text. Use only the part that helps you to prove your point.

- If your essay is mostly quotations from the text, it is not your essay. So, don't over-quote! Your job is not to string together phrases from the text. You are to use phrases from the text to prove your claims.

- Think about why you want to use the quoted phrase or passage in the first place. How does it support your claim? If you don't know, why are you quoting it?

- When quoting the text, set it up. You must give context first. If you find yourself "plopping" in a quotation and then explaining it, you have not provided the context.

USING PRECISE LANGUAGE: CONFIDENTLY SAYING WHAT YOU MEAN

- Use higher-level vocabulary

  I have suggested that you not toss in "big" words in your essays that you don't know. However, you still need to show that you have a sophisticated vocabulary. Begin to use the words you are learning from your word list in Chapter 9. If you never use a "big" word, your prose may sound simplistic.

- Use strong verbs

  Avoid using "being verbs" or linking verbs, as they do not express action. Instead choose strong, vivid action verbs. Your writing will be more powerful and more visual. When we write with linking and being verbs, we rely too much on adjectives. Adjectives can be vague or ambiguous. See the samples below.

Being/Linking Verbs			
is	are	have been	should have been
am	be	had been	would have been
was	been	shall be	feels
were	being	will be	seems

How do you know if it's an action verb? If you can act it out, it is an action verb. I can act out "dance," but I cannot act out "was."

Check your own writing for strong verb use. Choose any essay and highlight all the linking/being verbs you have used. Then, revise the essay and replace those highlighted verbs with action verbs. Notice the difference in the quality of your essay.

Below are some sample sentences that show the difference between using linking verbs and action verbs. Notice how much more vivid and descriptive the action verbs make the sentences.

Linking Verbs	Action Verbs
Sylvia was clumsy.	Sylvia tripped over the smallest pebble.
The images are interesting.	The images in the first paragraph evoke pity for the narrator.
The simile is effective.	The simile conjures images of wickedness.

WORDS AND PHRASES TO AVOID

Some words are inherently ambiguous. Others are simply meaningless. Others are cliché or overused expressions that are out of place in a scholarly essay. It is best to always avoid words and phrases that promote imprecision.

Avoid using:

- "Very," "really," "completely," etc. Superlatives added to adjectives are generally not needed.

- "Interesting." We all know that saying "that's interesting" can mean so many different things that it can actually mean nothing.

- "This," "that," and "it" can be ambiguity traps. It's best to not use them. For example: "That is why he never told even his closest friends about it." What is "that"? Furthermore, what is "it"?

- "Like," as in "the character was so like suffocated by his mother's dreams for him." Watch out for speech dysfluencies in writing. You are writing, not speaking.

- "Talks about" as in "This passage talks about." Passages do not talk. Instead say, the author writes, shows, reveals, etc.

- "Wonderful," "skillfully," "fantastic," when meant to compliment the writer. Do not "suck up" to the writer. This gains you no points. Praising the prose is not analyzing the prose.

NEVER, NEVER …

- Begin a sentence with a pronoun.

- Begin a paragraph with a pronoun.

- Use ambiguous pronouns: "this," "that," "those," "it," etc. If you need such a pronoun, it must be followed by the noun. Example This imagery….

- Write like you speak. That is, do not use a conversational style that screams out: "I am not serious."

- Use words you do not understand. If you misuse a word, you will lose credibility.

- Use more words than you need to use to make your point.

AVOID CLICHÉS, TRITE EXPRESSIONS, AND REDUNDANT PHRASES

If you've heard it before, it may be a cliché. Clichés are empty expressions that may have been clever at one time, but now simply distract from your writing. If you rely on clichés, you are avoiding your job as a writer, which is to use precise language to say what you mean.

A few common clichés:

- A close call
- A fish out of water
- At wit's end
- Bird's-eye view
- Coming down the pike
- Fall on deaf ears
- Long road to hoe
- Never a dull moment
- Nerve wracking
- Nipped in the bud
- Out of the box
- What goes around comes around
- At the end of the day

Redundant phrases:

- "At this point in time": just say *at this point* or *at this time*
- "Cancel out": just say *cancel*

- "Complete opposite": just say *opposite*
- "Each and every": just say *every*
- "Evolve over time": just say *evolve*
- "Join together": just say *join*
- "Look back in retrospect": just say *in retrospect*
- "Nostalgia for the past": just say *nostalgia*
- "Overexaggerate": just say *exaggerate*
- "Past experience": just say *experience*
- "Past history": just say *history*
- "Plan ahead": just say *plan*
- "The reason why": just say *the reason*
- "This day and age": just say *in our time* or *presently*
- "Ultimate goal": just say *goal*

YOUR OWN SYNTAX

You must be able to write effective and fluent sentences for effective prose. Just as the writers whose work is featured on the exam use syntactical patterns, so can you. Study these patterns (see Chapter 5) and learn the value of each. Practice writing various types of patterns. For example, one week, write just simple sentences, the next week compound, etc. This will result in your being able to use anaphora or polysyndeton without even thinking of how to do it, just knowing why you want to do it.

The best way to get better at sentence crafting is to recognize it in the texts you read and then emulate the patterns and effects you see.

Here is an activity to help you to practice writing better sentences and improve fluency.

Copy-change activity:
Make a copy of a highly effective paragraph from a book and study it. Learn the sentence patterns. Label the sentence types you see. Then, rewrite the paragraph with a new topic. Change the nouns and verbs to fit the new topic, but not their placement. Replicate phrases, clauses, and punctuation exactly. Learn by imitating.

Test Tip

YOUR OWN RHETORICAL STRATEGIES

Develop your paragraphs using a variety of rhetorical strategies. Use what seems appropriate for the text. In other words, you can't force something that doesn't work. Here are a few basic ways that you can argue your point.

Exemplification—Use examples from the text to prove your point. Of course, you will want to choose the best examples for your purpose.

Process analysis—If you recognize a process (how something works or operates) in a text, you can identify it and analyze its elements.

Comparison and contrast—Often, you will be asked to do this as your main task (such as compare two poems), but even if you aren't, you may have a reason to show similarities and differences in another type of question.

Cause-and-effect analysis—Show why something happens, the series of events leading to or causing a concluding event.

TWO TEXTS: A COMPARE/CONTRAST GUIDE

There is a good chance that you will be asked to write an essay comparing the elements of two texts. The following guide is meant to help you to understand the basics of compare/contrast essays.

The texts you will be presented with have some obvious similarities; otherwise, they would not be paired. You may have two poems about a Greek goddess or two descriptive paragraphs about shopping. The subjects will be the same. What will differ will be how the two authors treat the subjects. For example, the attitude of each author toward the subject may be completely different. It will be important for you to understand both overt and subtle similarities and differences. As you read, annotate the text and take marginal notes listing what you find.

Compare means to show similarities.

Contrast means to show differences.

COMPARE/CONTRAST: TRANSITIONAL WORDS AND PHRASES:

To compare

In the same way	Similarly	Like
Likewise	Also	

To contrast

Conversely	Rather	On the other hand
However	On the contrary	

THE INTRODUCTION

Mention both texts and be sure that your thesis suggests the main ways the two texts are similar. Do not say "Jones' poem is similar to Smith's in some ways, but there are also some main differences." Instead say, "Even though both poets characterize Venus as powerful, even fierce, Jones gives a sympathetic view of Venus, while Smith warns that her victims will be trapped by love."

THE BODY

Here are three popular methods you can use to organize the body of the essay:

1. With the "Whole to Whole" method you discuss the important aspects of one text, then the other.

   ‣ *You may lose track of your main points if you're not careful.*

2. Another method is to show all similarities, then all of the differences.

   ‣ *This can seem less integrated, less fluent.*

3. You might instead go subject by subject (point by point).

   ‣ *For example you might compare the tone in each poem, then the imagery in each poem, etc.*

ETHOS AND LOGOS:
TWO IMPORTANT ARGUMENT "TOOLS"

Aristotle defined qualities of argument centuries ago. Two terms of consequence for you are *ethos* and *logos*.

Ethos: The trustworthiness of the writer. You have to write what you know, what you believe, and support it well. Your essay will be voiceless and powerless if you don't believe in what you are saying. Your ethos is also shown in how credible your evidence is. Readers are likely to accept your argument if you have defended it well with appropriate evidence.

Logos: Using reason and logic to persuade. You must have a point to argue and know how to do it. You can use the rhetorical strategies listed above. Again, choosing the most appropriate evidence and arguing a clear, precise claim is your goal.

LEARNING FROM MODELS

Below is a sample essay written from an actual AP prompt. See Chapter 14 for more sample free response prompts and sample essays.

SAMPLE ESSAY

The following prompt is from an AP Lit exam.

> Read the following passage, from "A White Heron" by Sarah Orne Jewett, carefully. Then write an essay showing how the author dramatizes the young heroine's adventure. Consider such literary elements as diction, imagery, narrative pace, and point of view.

Key words in the prompt are "adventure" and "heroine." The prompt urges you to think of Sylvia's excursion in the old pine tree as a hero's journey. A list of literary elements is given. Diction and imagery are elements of any piece of literature, so those are not unexpected in the list. And while narrative pace and point of view are not uncommon, mentioning them specifically is a hint that they function specifically in this passage.

Do an online search for "A White Heron" by Sarah Orne Jewett. When you find the text, look for the first seven paragraphs in part II. The passage begins, "Half a mile from home, at the farther edge of the woods, where the land was highest, a great pine-tree stood, the last of its generation." The passage on the AP Lit exam was abridged from what you find here, but you will have a good sense of what students had as their text for this prompt.

In this excerpt from <u>A White Heron</u> by Sarah Orne Jewett,[1] the author takes us[2] on an adventurous journey with Sylvia, a small, but far from timid heroine, who shows that courage and tenacity can yield amazing results.[3] Jewett's imagery, diction and shift in point of view create an epic tale of a strong-willed little girl who climbs into a world she has previously only imagined to glimpse the wide world beyond her own.[4]

Jewett characterizes Sylvia as a "wistful" child who has long wondered about the old, lone pine tree "the last of its generation,"[5] believing that anyone who climbed it could see the ocean. Sylvia is a young heroine with an adventurous spirit who is filled with "wild ambition," a brave girl with "tingling, eager blood coursing the channels of her whole frame." While Sylvia is no stranger to climbing trees, the biggest tree she has previously explored is[6] the white oak whose "upper branches chafed against the pine trunk." She now knows she must go beyond the world she is familiar with and make "the dangerous pass from one tree to the other, so the great enterprise [can] really begin."

While the initial observations of Sylvia's character come through third person omniscient point of view, an interesting shift[7] occurs in the third

---

[1] Always mention title and author in the introduction.

[2] Example of universal first person.

[3] Alludes to the "so what," the universal and enduring theme prevalent in the passage.

[4] Thesis sentence

[5] Integrate only the parts of the text that support your claims. Weave them in so that your sentence is grammatically correct.

[6] Example of literary present tense.

[7] This claim recognizes a shift in point of view: something the prompt hinted would exist.

Overall, notice how the writer makes claims, gives textual evidence to support the claims, and explains what she means.

paragraph when the venerable tree becomes aware of his new tenant. Through the tree's perception of her, we further understand that Sylvia is "determined," "brave," "solitary," and of course "triumphant": all qualities of a hero on a journey.

The pine tree becomes an important character in Sylvia's adventure. He is like a "great main-mast to the voyaging earth," giving the impression that little Sylvia is on the greatest ship of all, sailing into her imagined world. The tree is first wary of his "visitor," who he sees as a "determined spark of human spirit creeping and climbing." But then he comes to appreciate her. While she is in his lower branches, he fights her, but as she continues in her journey, he comes to love his new dependent and even helps her along her way just as a mythical god might have helped humans he cared about; the tree reinforces his "least twigs," making them strong enough to hold her and holds "away the winds" so her last vantage point is steady.

Sylvia's adventure is in some ways comparable to epics of the past, and the lone pine tree provides the setting: it is a foreign land to be explored, full of obstacles, much like the lands beyond Ithaca in which Odysseus found his travails. Jewett's imagery and diction reinforces this idea. Sylvia begins her journey early in the morning "in the paling moonlight," a time when most people are still sleeping. The red squirrel "scolds" her as an unwelcomed stranger in his world. Jewett describes the treacherous climb up a tree that is like a "monstrous ladder," making it seem both tall and menacing. In addition, "sharp, dry twigs caught her and held her and scratched her like angry talons."[8] The trees twigs seem to be attacking Sylvia, like a bird of prey, creating a situation that requires her bravery and perseverance. Weaker spirits may have given up. Further advancing the idea that Sylvia is in a foreign land, Jewett writes in the third paragraph of the tree's usual

---

Evidence from the text can come from anywhere in the text. Quoted passages need not be in the order they were presented in the original text. Writers should use what they need to prove their points.

[8] Notice how the writer copes with a shift in verb tense. The text is in past, while this essay is in present tense. Learn to manage this difficulty so your prose is fluent.

The conclusion makes the essay feel complete, but it also reconnects with the "so what."

inhabitants: "hawks, bats, moths, and sweet-voiced thrushes," creatures that Sylvia would not generally associate with, but now she is in their territory and she can observe them closely.

Then Sylvia reaches the top of the pine tree, nestled in his loving branches. She is at the end of her journey. To see her now from below, she seems like a "pale star," almost as if she's part of heaven instead of earth. Jewett exalts her tiny heroine at last. What Sylvia sees finally is truly majestic and a reward for her courage and determination. The golden sun shines on the sea. The hawks are so close that she recognizes how slowly their wings move, and she sees their feathers as gray and "soft as moths," details she never could have detected while on the ordinary earth.

Sylvia's reward is a new view of her own world that may make her feel both small and daring. Like all of us who venture beyond what is familiar and comfortable,[9] she realizes that the world is larger and more vast than she realized. But she must also know that she is ready for any journey her future brings. Unlike more timid spirits, Sylvia's courage and tenacity will reward her with the joys of new discoveries.

---

[9] Sylvia's journey is a metaphor for all of us: push beyond what is familiar and be rewarded for our courage.

Avoid clichés: "comfort zone," "outside the box," etc.

An Analytical Approach
to Essay Improvement

"What we have to learn to do, we learn by doing."

—Aristotle

OVERVIEW

In the same way that we learn to ride a bike or play a piano or shoot a basket—by repeating the process, by doing it again and again until we understand it—we learn to write by writing. Writing AP essays is a skill you can learn to do well. However, you must devote time to practice. You cannot learn to write good essays simply by reading this book. This book gives you the guidelines and the tools to use. To improve, you must actually *practice* writing.

STUDYING SAMPLE STUDENT ESSAYS

Every year, the College Board publishes sample student essays for each free-response question. The questions are scored at three levels: high, medium, and low. By recognizing why each essay was scored as it was, you can learn both what to do and what not to do.

The following table gives you an idea of what you will see when you go to the AP Central website. Each item in the cells below will be found at that site. I have numbered each item and explained below what you will find when you click on the link. The information given will vary from year to year. The most important elements are 1, 2, and 5.

2018: FREE-RESPONSE QUESTIONS

Questions	Scoring	Samples and Commentary	Score Distributions
Free-Response Questions	Scoring Guidelines Chief Reader Report Scoring Statistics	Sample Responses Q1 Sample Responses Q2 Sample Responses Q3	Scoring Distributions

1. "Free-Response Questions" are the actual questions for that specific year and the texts on which they were based. Often there are two different tests for a given year, which means you have twice as many samples from which to learn. The second test will be labeled *Form B*.

2. "Scoring Guidelines" is a document that the AP readers were given prior to scoring each essay. It is their rubric.

3. "Chief Reader Report" is a document geared toward AP teachers, but you will find it illuminating as well.

The document is a summary of what the intent of each question was, what they were hoping students would do with each question, the average scores, the main problems they witnessed in student essays, and tips for teachers to help students to do better in the future.

4. "Scoring Statistics" shows how most students scored on the essays; it gives you the mean score. Most students typically score in the middle range on their essays.

5. For each question (Q1, 2, and 3) you will get three student essays. There is always a top-rated essay, a middle one, and a lower rated essay. Look for what makes the top essay different from the middle or lower essay. You will also find a summary of readers' commentaries here. This information can be enlightening, as what they have to say often reinforces what you are learning about writing good essays. Do read and take to heart what they say in the commentary.

6. The College Board periodically publishes score distributions. This report shows you how many students scored a 5, a 4, and so on. It does not tell you specifically about how students scored on any particular essay, but only for the exam in general. This is the least meaningful bit of information here, and regarding your goal to improve your essays, is not all that helpful.

In your analysis, you will want to specifically look for the following:

1) What did the prompt ask students to do?

2) How effective was the particular student's introduction?

3) How did the writer follow the method of stating a claim, defending it with evidence from the text, and explaining what he or she meant (CECT)?

4) In high-scoring essays, look for the way the writer embedded evidence from the text.

5) Look for his or her use of transitions from one point to the next and from the claim to the support.

6) Note how a writer took the argument beyond ordinary (see Chapter 11).

METHOD FOR ANALYZING SAMPLE STUDENT ESSAYS

The following worksheet was designed to help you to analyze sample student essays for their strengths and weaknesses. By using the worksheet you can see where you need to go with your own writing. This process does take time, but your deliberate work here will be illuminating.

Test Tip

It would be worth your time to repeat this analysis process several times until you clearly see the qualities of top essays versus their less effective counterparts.

The steps of the process are:

Part 1:

1. Read and analyze the prompt for one question. (Don't use question 3 because no text is given for you to read.)

2. Paraphrase the task.

3. Read and annotate the passage.

4. Suggest literary devices, if needed.

    5. Write your own introduction, for practice.

    6. Write a mini-outline for the essay that you would write —if you were asked to write it.

Part 2:

    1. Read and score each of the three essays.

    2. Justify your score.

Part 3:

    1. Compare your score with the actual score that was given.

    2. Read the commentary for each essay.

    3. Draw your own conclusions.

You will find everything you need for this exercise at the AP Central site: *https://apcentral.collegeboard.org.*

You may choose any year, but it might be best to start with a recent year to get a prompt that indicates current College Board thinking.

PDF documents you will need to print:

- Click on the "All Questions" link and print (all of the texts and prompts are here).

- Choose one question (not question 3) and print the "Sample Responses" for that question. Do not read this document until told to do so.

- Print "Scoring Guidelines."

[*Note*: You have permission from REA to make copies of the following chart for your personal use.]

PART ONE: UNDERSTANDING THE PROMPT AND YOUR TASK

1. Begin by reading the prompt for any essay question. (Do not use the prompt for question three.) Underline the verbs that direct your task. Circle the thematic focus (the "so-what").

2. Paraphrase the task:

3. Read the passage, annotating it for anything that seems significant, especially in light of the prompt.

4. If your prompt does not suggest literary devices, make a list of what you think are the most important devices here:

5. Practice: Write an introduction as if you were going to write this essay.

6. Create a mini-outline of your main points.

PART TWO: ANALYZING STUDENT SAMPLES

For this part, you will need the "Scoring Guidelines."

Read each of the essays, score each separately, and justify your score (say why you gave each the score you did).

Important!!! Promise not to read the scores or commentaries for each essay until part 3.

Essay # _____

Score: _____

Justification:

Essay # _____

Score: _____

Justification:

Essay # _____

Score: _____

Justification:

PART THREE: COMPARING SCORES

For this part, you will need the commentaries (at the end of the essay document).

Essay #	My Score/ I gave	The Score/ AP readers gave	Observations

PART FOUR: CONCLUSIONS

What did you learn from this analysis?

Sample Free-Response Questions and Essays

1. (SUGGESTED TIME: 40 MINUTES)

In the following excerpt from Sherwood Anderson's story "Departure" a young man prepares for a journey away from home. In a well-organized essay, analyze how diction, imagery, and selection of details help to convey George Willard's state of mind as he prepares to board the train.

Line

Young George Willard got out of bed at four in the morning. It was April and the young tree leaves were just coming out of their buds. The trees along the residence streets in Winesburg are maple and the seeds are winged. When the wind blows they whirl crazily

(5) about, filling the air and making a carpet underfoot.

George came downstairs into the hotel office carrying a brown leather bag. His trunk was packed for departure. Since two o'clock he had been awake thinking of the journey he was about to take and wondering what he would find at the end of his journey. The

(10) boy who slept in the hotel office lay on a cot by the door. His mouth was open and he snored lustily. George crept past the cot and went out into the silent deserted main street. The east was pink with the dawn and long streaks of light climbed into the sky where a few stars still shone.

(15) Beyond the last house on Trunion Pike in Winesburg there is a great stretch of open fields. The fields are owned by farmers who live in town and drive homeward at evening along Trunion Pike in light creaking wagons. In the fields are planted berries and small

fruits. In the late afternoon in the hot summers when the road and
(20)   the fields are covered with dust, a smoky haze lies over the great
flat basin of land. To look across it is like looking out across the sea.
In the spring when the land is green the effect is somewhat different. The land becomes a wide green billiard table on which tiny
human insects toil up and down.

(25)   All through his boyhood and young manhood George Willard
had been in the habit of walking on Trunion Pike. He had been in
the midst of the great open place on winter nights when it was
covered with snow and only the moon looked down at him; he
had been there in the fall when bleak winds blew and on sum-
(30)   mer evenings when the air vibrated with the song of insects. On
the April morning he wanted to go there again, to walk again in
the silence. He did walk to where the road dipped down by a little
stream two miles from town and then turned and walked silently
back again. When he got to Main Street clerks were sweeping the
(35)   sidewalks before the stores. "Hey, you George. How does it feel to
be going away?" they asked.

The westbound train leaves Winesburg at seven forty-five in the
morning. Tom Little is conductor. His train runs from Cleveland to
where it connects with a great trunk line railroad with terminals in
(40)   Chicago and New York. Tom has what in railroad circles is called an
"easy run." Every evening he returns to his family. In the fall and
spring he spends his Sundays fishing in Lake Erie. He has a round
red face and small blue eyes. He knows the people in the towns
along his railroad better than a city man knows the people who
(45)   live in his apartment building.

George came down the little incline from the New Willard
House at seven o'clock. Tom Willard carried his bag. The son had
become taller than the father.

On the station platform everyone shook the young man's hand.
(50)   More than a dozen people waited about. Then they talked of their
own affairs. Even Will Henderson, who was lazy and often slept
until nine, had got out of bed. George was embarrassed. Gertrude

Wilmot, a tall thin woman of fifty who worked in the Winesburg post office, came along the station platform. She had never before
(55) paid any attention to George. Now she stopped and put out her hand. In two words she voiced what everyone felt. "Good luck," she said sharply and then turning went on her way.

from *Winesburg, Ohio (1919)*, Sherwood Anderson's collection of stories about life in a small town at the end of the nineteenth century.

2. (SUGGESTED TIME: 40 MINUTES)

Carefully read the following two poems. In each, the poet personifies a natural element as female. In a well-organized essay compare and contrast how each poet characterizes her subject and her role in nature. Be sure to consider how each poet employs imagery and figurative language in her purpose.

To an Early Daffodil

Line

Thou yellow trumpeter of laggard Spring!
Thou herald of rich Summer's myriad flowers!
The climbing sun with new recovered powers
Does warm thee into being, through the ring
(5) Of rich, brown earth he woos thee, makes thee fling
Thy green shoots up, inheriting the dowers[1]
Of bending sky and sudden, sweeping showers,
Till ripe and blossoming thou art a thing
To fill the lonely with a joy untold;
(10) Nodding at every gust of wind to-day,
To-morrow jewelled with raindrops. Always bold
To stand erect, full in the dazzling play
Of April's sun, for thou hast caught his gold.

by Amy Lowell, from *A Dome of Many-Coloured Glass*

---

[1] Dowers: a dower is the property settled on the bride herself by the groom at the time of marriage.

A Solar Eclipse

In that great journey of the stars through space
About the mighty, all-directing Sun,
The pallid, faithful Moon, has been the one
Companion of the Earth. Her tender face,
(5) Pale with the swift, keen purpose of that race,
Which at Time's natal hour was first begun,
Shines ever on her lover as they run
And lights his orbit with her silvery smile.

Sometimes such passionate love doth in her rise,
(10) Down from her beaten path she softly slips,
And with her mantle veils the Sun's bold eyes,
Then in the gloaming finds her lover's lips.
While far and near the men our world call wise
See only that the Sun is in eclipse.

by Ella Wheeler Wilcox

3. (SUGGESTED TIME: 40 MINUTES)

American fiction writer Jhumpa Lahiri offers this observation
about literature:

> "From the beginnings of literature, poets and writers have based
> their narratives on crossing borders, on wandering, on exile, on
> encounters beyond the familiar. The stranger is an archetype in epic
> poetry, in novels. The tension between alienation and assimilation
> has always been a basic theme."

Choose a novel or play that features an exiled or alienated
protagonist. In a well-written essay, characterize the protagonist's
alienation as well as how the character emerges from "the tension
between alienation and assimilation" evident in the ending and
explain its significance in the work as a whole.

You may select a work from the list below or another novel or play of literary merit.

1984	*King Lear*
A Lesson Before Dying	*Moby Dick*
A Portrait of the Artist as a Young Man	*Native Son*
	Song of Solomon
A Raisin in the Sun	*The Color Purple*
Adventures of Huckleberry Finn	*The Crucible*
All the Pretty Horses	*The Handmaid's Tale*
Ceremony	*The Heart is a Lonely Hunter*
Cry, the Beloved Country	*The Lovesong of J. Alfred Prufrock*
Emma	
Great Expectations	*The Sun Also Rises*
Heart of Darkness	*The Tempest*
House Made of Dawn	*Their Eyes Were Watching God*
Invisible Man	*To Kill a Mockingbird*
Jane Eyre	

DISCLAIMER ON THE FOLLOWING SAMPLE ESSAYS:

AP readers and teachers will tell you that the essay you write in about 40 minutes for your exam is considered a draft. A perfected essay is not what they're looking for. What they are looking for is for you to be able to write well enough to articulate a thoughtful and well-defended analysis. The essays that follow were written initially within the 40-minute time constraints. However, to make these essays suitable to publish and serve as models, extra time was spent to revise and structure them accordingly.

Additionally, the essays that follow present just one writer's response. We do not suggest these essays stand as the "right answer." Surely other ideas that could be equally well developed occurred to you as you read the texts and prompts.

Models written by actual students for the previous year's exam are readily available to you on the AP Central website.

Test Tip *Use the prompt given for Question 3 and write an essay using one of the other titles listed. If you are part of a study group, suggest everyone do the same. Then share and critique each other's essays.*

SAMPLE ESSAY RESPONSE: QUESTION 1

In this excerpt from his story "Departure," Sherwood Anderson[2] presents George Willard, a young man from a small town who rises early in anticipation[3] of a momentous life journey, a journey celebrated by nature and blessed by everyone George knows.

The morning comes early for George on the day of his departure. He is clearly anxious to begin as he awakes at two, unable to sleep as he thinks of his journey. When, at four a.m., he can no longer lie in bed, George rises and walks the deserted streets of Winesburg. This walk about, a kind of goodbye trek, allows Anderson to show George's home as well as hint at the young man's future.

Anderson presents, through George's perspective, images of the town and the fields that lay beyond.[4] Such imagery suggests George longs to know what lies beyond his own inland seas.[5] Anderson describes "a great flat basin of land" that even in winter and covered by snow is a "great open space." Beyond George's family home, Ohio opens up, and "to look

---

[2] The writer acknowledges the author and the name of the work.

[3] As the prompt asks, this writer identifies George's state of mind: anticipation.

[4] The first paragraph cites details from the excerpt that show George's overt anxiety and anticipation.

[5] In this paragraph, the writer infers George may long to see an ocean and presents evidence to support this inference.

across it is like looking out across a sea." Such imagery stands in sharp contrast to George's comfortable home in the local hotel his family owns, which also suggests that while anxious to leave, George may also be intimidated[6] by the vast unknown before him.

Anderson's imagery and selection of detail provide an auspicious morning for George Willard as nature itself welcomes George on the morning of his journey. Anderson sets the scene in April, the archetypical month for rebirth and renewal in life. The early dawn is described as "pink," making "long streaks of light, climbing in the sky," surely an allusion[7] to Homer whose "rosy-fingered dawn" greeted Odysseus as he began his long journey home. Even George's footsteps are granted ease by the fallen maple seeds that blow about him and make a "carpet underfoot."

Anderson uses imagery again to underscore a tone of excitement. He presents the maple seeds that "whirl crazily about" and says the air "vibrated with the song of insects." Even the "lusty snoring" of the office boy sleeping on his cot adds an anticipatory buzz to the air.[8]

The town itself anticipates a great journey for George, whom the townspeople see, perhaps, as their emissary into the wider world. In colloquial diction, one Main Street clerk says, "Hey, You, George" and asks how it feels to be going away. To underscore what a big deal this event is for those in Winesburg, even "lazy" Will Henderson who "often slept till nine" gets out of bed purposefully to see George off and a woman who "had never before paid any attention to George" wishes him good luck.

Just as other young explorers before him, George is headed west, the symbolic direction of discovery. However, instead of seeking the Wild West, there is every indication that George will seek out a city on his journey.

---

[6] This claim reconnects with dictate of the prompt, to explore George's "state of mind" and expands on the idea.

[7] This writer has noticed Anderson's use of a symbolic archetype and allusion to Homer's *Odyssey* (a classic heroic journey story) to reinforce the importance of George's own journey.

[8] Staying on task, the writer presents more evidence that Anderson's imagery creates an anxious feeling in the excerpt.

Anderson says the westbound train connects eventually "with terminals in Chicago and New York."[9]

Finally[10], in a small but sharp detail, George's father carries his son's bag, which suggests George has his father's blessing. If there is sadness in seeing his son depart, it comes from the other detail Anderson shares about the father-son relationship, and that is that George has "become taller" than his father. This detail suggests maturity rather than simple height and proves the son is no longer a child.

Like so many other young people who find it is time at last to leave home and their parents to see what the world is all about, George is ready. However, if he should ever want to come home, the train is an "easy run," which nightly brings the conductor himself back to his family.[11]

SAMPLE ESSAY RESPONSE: QUESTION 2

In "To an Early Daffodil," Amy Lowell presents a female daffodil and gives her the charge of trumpeting the arrival of spring. This flower is also to be the "herald" that announces the arrival of all the other flowers who follow her. While her job is important, Lowell's daffodil is less powerful and less self-determined than her counterpart[12] in "A Solar Eclipse" by Ella Wheeler Wilcox, a female moon who holds the power in her relationship with the earth, even to the point of being able to eclipse the sun for her own need.

---

[9] In this paragraph, the writer uses details from the work to not only suggest George's destination but to also show that by using west as a direction, Anderson once again relies on iconic symbolism.

[10] A simple transition signals the writer's last point.

[11] In the conclusion to this essay, instead of a generic summary conclusion, the writer reinforces the idea that George's journey is a natural aspect of youth, but also conveys the comforting notion that home is never far away by making reference to the train conductor's ability to come home each night.

[12] The prompt asks writers to characterize each poet's subject and her role in nature. This writer points out that the daffodil is less powerful and less self-determined than her counterpart, the moon, which sets up a contrast to develop.

Both poets use[13] figurative language in their primary metaphors—a love relationship. In the Lowell poem, the daffodil is being wooed by the sun, while in the Wilcox poem, the moon is in love with the earth. Words like "woo," "dowers," "even "ring" aid Lowell in suggesting a wedding between the sun and the daffodil. The sun, as god of the skies, owns the "showers" which he gifts to his bride. In the Wilcox poem, the moon's relationship with the earth is presented as a timeless and monogamous relationship. The moon is the earth's "one companion." Wilcox's metaphor is direct and terms like "passionate" and "lover's lips" make the moon's feelings of love explicit.

[14]Clearly the moon is the stronger of the two females. She is not as transient as the daffodil who comes once each spring. The moon has been the steadfast "companion of the earth" since time's "natal hour," or since time began. Not only is the moon older, she is also able to act on her own passion by "softly slip[ping]" from her orbit to kiss "her lover's lips." The moon also has the power to conceal her act by "veil[ing]"[15] the sun's bold eyes." The daffodil on the other hand, while she plays an important role as spring's official messenger or "herald," must be given her office by her lover, the sun, who woos and warms her into existence. The daffodil also is given her wedding gifts or "dowers," such as the sun and the rain. Eventually, she will blossom, but instead of steering her own timeless purpose as the moon does, the daffodil is given her power to provide "joy untold" to lonely humans by her "husband," the sun.

Imagery,[16] particularly in the use of color in each poem serves to cast a fitting light for each heroine, uplifting the beauty of each. Lowell colors her poem vibrantly in yellow, brown, green, and gold, colors of a spring day itself. Within that palette, yellow and gold overtake the others, and their

---

[13] Use language that shows comparisons and contrasts while also directly stating a claim. In this case, the writer is saying both poets use a similar primary metaphor.

[14] The next two paragraphs, each on their own, discuss how the poets characterize the power or inherent strength of each subject. These paragraphs are used in direct support of this writer's thesis.

[15] When citing the text, it is sometimes necessary to change tense in order to be grammatically correct and fluent.

[16] As asked by the prompt, this writer considers the effect of imagery and narrows the analysis to colors used and the effect of the colors. Responding to at least one of the suggested literary elements (if available) is desirable.

prominence is aided by words like "jewelled" and "dazzling," which suggest the daffodil exudes light. Further, the daffodil catches the sun's gold, implying she can shine as brightly as he does. In contrast, Wilcox draws on a quieter, paler image, saying the moon, whose "tender face [is] pale" has a "silvery smile." In this color scheme, the sun's brightness is effectively dimmed so the moon can take prominence. Terms like "mantle veils" and "gloaming" allow Wilcox to create a shadowy effect.

[17] While both the daffodil and the moon are personified as beautiful, only the moon possesses steadfast self-determination. The daffodil's strength is subtler and more passive, as she is given her very existence from her husband, though in the end, she does take from the sun his gold. The sun plays a different role in the Wilcox poem. The sun, not the moon, is the object of human interest. Ironically, the fault in the wise men's logic only serves the poet in amplifying her heroine's great power.

SAMPLE ESSAY RESPONSE: QUESTION 3

In Twain's *The Adventures of Huckleberry Finn*, the protagonist Huckleberry Finn, perhaps American literature's most iconic orphan, stands both as an observer of a corrupt American society and as a beacon for how we ought to live in a more modern, enlightened world. It is precisely Huck's alienation that allows him to covertly observe the world as well as provides him a credible voice. His wise observances throughout the novel set up the end, where he questions whether or not he wishes to be assimilated.[18]

While not technically an orphan, as Huck's pap is still alive early in the novel, Huck has been effectively alienated from society by the ill treatment and neglect of his drunken, bigoted, and abusive father. For a time,

---

[17] The conclusion to this essay breaks from a generic summary conclusion. While the writer does reinforce a key idea from the introduction, she goes beyond and qualifies the power of the daffodil and the moon, suggesting the moon is a supreme being.

[18] The introduction clearly states the title of the work used for the essay, the author of the work, as well as the character used in example. The writer also alludes to the given task, to analyze a character who is caught in "the tension between alienation and assimilation." The writer alludes to the point that will eventually be made: the protagonist will not assimilate by the novel's end.

Huck is "rescued" by the Widow Douglas and Miss Watson, who try their best to provide for Huck. By society's gauge, Huck—now dressed in proper clothes and eating regular meals, even receiving religious instruction—is finally living as he rightly ought to be. And yet Huck chafes at being reintegrated into normal life.[19] Even the normal activities of boys his age, such as Tom's robber gang, seem frivolous to Huck. While Tom fantasizes he's an outlaw, Huck has had to scrabble to survive. Huck's pap is truly an outlaw, and that life is not a game to Huck. After all the good intentions of the widow and Judge Thatcher to protect him and his interests, Huck prefers to live on his own, so when the opportunity presents itself, he fakes his death and effectively becomes more alienated than ever before.

Once Huck begins to experience life away from social expectations, he is free to establish his own set of standards. Joined by runaway slave Jim, the two float peacefully downriver on a raft. For a time, they answer to no one but themselves. It is in this section of the novel that Twain's most beautiful descriptions of nature—the river, the night sky, the sounds of steamboats passing—put human life into perspective. Ugliness is replaced by beauty. Through his stories, Jim teaches Huck about life and Huck begins to consider what is right, what is wise, and what is love. Huck begins to see Jim as a man and a grieving father, not just as a slave. And yet, their idyllic life on the raft cannot last. Jim is not free, and his need to find his family places Huck in the position of having to choose between what society expects from him and what his heart tells him is right.

Apart from society, Huck's episodic journey down the Mississippi teaches him what no book or school lesson could teach. Apart from what Huck learns from Jim, he sees through observation that the world is often ugly, often ridiculous. Life away from the raft is teeming with violence and corruption. From the feuding Shepherdsons and Grangerfords to lowlife grifters like the king and the duke, Huck encounters very few heroic people on shore. Even the safety of the river is compromised by slave traders on the lookout for runaways.

---

[19] Throughout the essay, the writer makes reference to episodes or events in the novel that show Huckleberry Finn to be caught between two worlds. The writer never summarizes for its own sake, but tells about parts of the novel in order to make a point about Huck's alienation. Further, reasons for Huck's alienation are presented and clarified.

In the most important scene in the novel, Huck decides to "go to hell" for Jim, choosing to help his friend and keep him safe no matter what the law says. In thinking he's doing wrong, Huck chooses to break completely from the laws of his society, which ironically lifts him as a moral paradigm. Also ironic is the fact that in order to protect Jim, Huck must lie and steal, but readers understand these illegal actions are always in the service of his higher moral purpose. It's Huck's moral strength that makes him a beacon for society. Some laws are unjust and right-thinking people must oppose them, even if doing so puts them in legal jeopardy.

After Huck turns his back on society's ingrained but flawed ways, he realizes that he will never be able to re-integrate. At the end of the novel, even after Huck learns he would be welcomed by his relatives, particularly Aunt Sally who wants to "sivilize" him, he is unwilling to re-join their world. He figures he has seen enough of civilization as it exists. When Huck says he will "light out for the Territory ahead,"[20] he means to seek a different path. Surely Twain hoped his readers would see Huck as a hero who emerges out of ignorance into truth. The once lost boy finds his own way, his own lights, bright enough for all to follow.

---

[20] An exact quotation from the work is never expected for Question 3, but if a line or two is memorable or apt, use it.

Summary of Essay Tips

"Mature writing recognizes and explores the ambiguities and ironies that plague human existence."

— Note in the Student Performance Q&A,
AP Central website (2007)

In This Chapter

Overview	Questions 1 and 2
Essays in General	Question 3

OVERVIEW

This chapter summarizes the information found in earlier chapters and specifically reiterates things you must remember. You can be sure that these are important enough to study again and again. The more you remember these tips and strategies and the more you integrate them into how you think about your own writing and thinking processes, the fewer problems you will encounter when writing your essays for the AP Lit exam.

ESSAYS IN GENERAL

- Read the prompt carefully and answer it, attending to all elements of the prompt. Be sure you understand what you are being asked to do.

- Rewriting the prompt on your paper is a waste of your time. Your introduction and thesis will acknowledge that you understand all elements of the prompt.

- Saying the same thing again and again does not strengthen your point.

- An essay can be a draft but it still must be a coherent whole— not a string of disconnected ideas.

- Move from "what" to "why" and "how." Show how literary devices contribute to the meaning of the text.

- Explain fully and support your claims. Do not write in short "sound bites."

- Use the literary present tense. Characters in literature are always alive. They live in the present time of the text.

- Avoid second person ("you"); write primarily in third person, using first as needed (if needed). Third person is a more authoritative voice.

- Never use qualifying phrases like "I think," "I feel," or "In my opinion." The claims you make in your essay belong to no one else but you. Such phrases make you sound less confident.

- Avoid new analysis in the conclusion. The conclusion is meant to provide a finish or end to your essay, not to raise another point.

- Do not define a literary element, such as tone or irony. Your readers are fully aware of the meanings of all literary elements.

- Never provide a summary of the plot or the action of the work.

QUESTIONS 1 AND 2 (POETRY AND PROSE PROMPTS)

- Some prompts may give you a list of literary elements or techniques to consider for your argument, but some may not. If there is no list, then you are expected to know what literary techniques are significant.

- Do not be a tour guide. Even though the prompt may give you a list of literary elements to explore, it's not your job to take your reader on a tour of the text, pointing out this example of imagery or that metaphor. Instead, focus on one or two elements that are most effective and show how they are effective. This is your analysis.

- Do not write about a literary element if it's not working toward the purpose or effect in the text. For example, rhyme is rarely a significant element in a poem. If you say it is, then it is your job to show how or why.

- Poems are short and therefore students may think simple. However, poems are laden with figurative language. Do not mistake the figurative for the literal. Read poems at least twice to be able to write intelligently.

QUESTION 3 (OPEN-ENDED QUESTION FOR WHICH YOU WILL CHOOSE A NOVEL OR PLAY)

- You must choose a work that fits the question. Choose carefully. Your best choice will probably come from the list of works provided. They are there for a reason—they are all examples of a book or play that fits the question.

- The list of works given for question three is not meant to constrain you and you may choose any other work of equal literary merit. Be very careful in your choice. You will seriously jeopardize your chance of earning a high score if AP readers think the book is not quality literature.

- Do not think that AP readers are unfamiliar with a text you choose. There are hundreds of readers and even if you choose something you think is obscure, someone will be familiar with it.

- Do not use the movie version of a text. You have to read the book (play). If it is clear that you're referring to the movie version, you'll lose points.

- You need to be familiar with details of plot and character. You need to know who's who and their relationships to one another.

- You will be expected to provide specific details from the text. While it is not fair to expect direct quotations, it is fair to expect specific references. Use the graphic organizer in Chapter 4 to record details of plot, character, theme and more for five to seven texts that you know very well. While you won't be able to use these self-made guides on the exam, the act of creating them will help you store what you need to know in your long-term memory.

- A plot summary is not an argument—if you write a summary, you're going to get a very low score.

PART V:

MASTERING THE MULTIPLE-CHOICE SECTION

Strategies for Success
on the Multiple-Choice Section

"The beginning of knowledge is the discovery of something we do not understand."

—Frank Herbert

In This Chapter

Overview

Strategic Reading

Use the Questions to Take the Test

Tips on Answering Questions

Practice for Real

OVERVIEW

To quote the College Board, the multiple-choice section of the exam "includes excerpts from several published works of drama, poetry, or prose fiction. Each excerpt is accompanied by several multiple-choice questions or prompts." There are typically 55 questions in all.

You've been taking standardized tests since you were in elementary school, and no one knows more about test taking than a high school student. However, the stakes for this exam are higher than others you've taken, so it seems appropriate to review the skills and strategies needed to answer multiple-choice questions. Some of what you find in this chapter will seem familiar, as if you've read it in other chapters. But these tips bear repeating.

You will want to have these strategies ingrained in your brain. Just the very nature of the test day can bring stress. You should not have to worry about a "guessing" strategy. Use this chapter in combination with Chapter 20, "Types of Multiple-Choice Questions," to ensure your best possible score for the multiple-choice section of the exam.

STRATEGIC READING

Before you answer the first question on the test, you must carefully read passages taken from novels or expository prose or poems. The smart way to read is to *read actively*. Active reading means that you read with a pen in hand, underlining key ideas, writing notes in the margin, connecting related thoughts and so on. Using your pen actively as you read will help you to be fully focused on what you are reading. It will help you to avoid the distraction that can cause your mind to wander. If you practice active reading, you should only need to read an entire prose text once. However, it is advisable to read poems at least twice. Poetry presents difficulties due to figurative language and indirect expression.

Whether you read a text once or twice, remember to read actively. Use whatever annotation techniques you are comfortable with, but do mark the text as you read. This process of close and active reading will help you remember what you've read and will help you identify key aspects of a particular text.

What to note/mark:

- Circle and link related words. For example, five words with a sarcastic tone in a passage are worth noting.

- Underline key statements (anything that seems to be significant).

- Any shift in speaker, point of view, tone, or purpose is important to note in the margin. Also jot down what you think is happening because of this shift.

- Write your own questions in the margin, even questions as simple as "why?" or "what does this mean?" Your questions help you to think and may be answered as you read further, which will provide a logical link for you.

USE THE QUESTIONS TO TAKE THE TEST

- Test questions may provide insight into the poem/passage and improve your reading comprehension.

- Skimming the test questions before you read can give you a stronger purpose for reading and will help you annotate the text as you read. But do skim quickly. You do not have time to carefully read all the questions first.

TIPS ON ANSWERING QUESTIONS

- While it sounds like common sense, read questions carefully. Be sure you know what a question is asking. Cursory reading creates careless errors. See Chapter 20 for an analysis of question types.

- Cross out answers that you know are wrong.

- Many of the really tough questions provide two similar answers that you think are correct. In this case, you must choose the most correct answer. "Most correct" means *the answer is more precise or more detailed.* If another answer is only "sort of" right, then that is most likely the wrong choice.

- Don't overthink a question. Some questions are really, really easy. Many students think such an easy question couldn't possibly be on the exam, so they overthink it and get it wrong.

- If you really don't know the answer, but can eliminate two or more answers, taking a guess might be better than skipping the question. You've already eliminated two answers so you have a far better chance of guessing right!

- If the question asks you to identify ironic elements, the statement in the answer will reveal the irony. In other words, the answer itself will sound ironic.

- For EXCEPT questions, look for the one thing that doesn't match the others.

- Many questions require a rereading of lines or paragraphs from the text. Do not avoid this step. Your annotation notes and markings of the text should help you navigate the text more efficiently as you reread.

PRACTICE FOR REAL

After reading and studying this book, you can get some AP test experience by taking our online AP English Literature and Composition practice test available at *www.rea.com/studycenter*.

After taking the practice exam, analyze your results. When you review your answers, ask two questions:

1. Why did I get it right?

2. Why did I get it wrong?

It is just as important for you to understand what you got right as well as what you got wrong. If any topics seem particularly difficult, review them now. Study this *Crash Course* along with your textbook and you'll be all set when test day rolls around.

Look through any practice exam for literary terms you are not familiar with or words you do not understand. Add them to your "to do" list and learn them.

Types of Questions in the Multiple-Choice Section

In This Chapter

Overview

Types of Questions by Purpose

OVERVIEW

The following information comes from an analysis of released AP Lit exams. Questions are organized according to purpose.

TYPES OF QUESTIONS BY PURPOSE

GENERAL ANALYSIS QUESTIONS:

1. Determine the purpose or function or rhetorical purpose — of a sentence or phrase or clause or word.

2. Draw a general conclusion or make an inference or logical deduction — from a line or group of lines or word(s).

3. Determine the effect of the speaker or character's attitude. The variations of this question include

analysis of speaker's beliefs, assumptions, and perceptions.

4. Determine an element of characterization: how a person, thing, idea, etc., is characterized.

5. Give a general interpretation or conclusion. These questions test your general reading comprehension.

6. Which lines are closest in meaning to or are the best restatement of a phrase or group of lines?

7. Determine the primary effect or purpose or rhetorical function of a passage or section.

8. Identify the central rhetorical strategy used in the passage.

9. Determine the effect of a rhetorical shift.

ORGANIZATION AND STRUCTURE QUESTIONS:

1. Identify compared/contrasted elements. The question is often worded, "Which best contrasts with _____?" The question may also ask you to determine the effect of the contrast or comparison. These compare/contrast questions are often layered with other question types.

2. Identify a method of organization in a passage or paragraph.

3. Identify a critical transition point and its effect.

4. Identify a cause/effect relationship in the passage or paragraph.

5. Give an analysis of the relationship between structural elements, such as paragraphs, lines, or sections.

SENTENCE AND SYNTAX QUESTIONS:

1. Give an analysis of syntactic patterns or sentence effects.

2. Give an analysis of repetition elements.

GRAMMATICAL CONSTRUCTION QUESTIONS:

1. Make a grammatical connection, such as "the word or phrase refers to _____." On occasion you are asked to find a word's antecedent.

2. Identify what it is that a phrase or clause modifies.

DENOTATION AND CONNOTATION QUESTIONS:

1. Which is the best interpretation of a phrase?

2. Determine the effect of the diction.

LITERARY ANALYSIS QUESTIONS:

1. Directly identify a literary element or determine the effect of a particular literary element.

2. Determine the effect of imagery or a description.

3. Analyze an element of figurative language.

4. Determine the effect of an allusion.

5. Determine the mood or tone of a passage or phrase.

6. Determine the ironic elements.

7. Identify the style of a paragraph.

Practice Multiple-Choice Questions

Practice with the following AP-style questions. Then go online to access a timed, full-length practice exam at *www.rea.com/studycenter*.

Questions 1–5. Read the following poem carefully before you choose your answers.

To an Early Daffodil

Line

Thou yellow trumpeter of laggard Spring!
Thou herald of rich Summer's myriad flowers!
The climbing sun with new recovered powers
Does warm thee into being, through the ring
(5) Of rich, brown earth he woos thee, makes thee fling
Thy green shoots up, inheriting the dowers[1]
Of bending sky and sudden, sweeping showers,
Till ripe and blossoming thou art a thing
To fill the lonely with a joy untold;
(10) Nodding at every gust of wind to-day,
To-morrow jewelled with raindrops. Always bold
To stand erect, full in the dazzling play
Of April's sun, for thou hast caught his gold.

by Amy Lowell, from *A Dome of Many-Coloured Glass*

1. Which literary device is evident in the title?

   (A) simile

   (B) personification

   (C) apostrophe

   (D) metonymy

   (E) ode

---

[1] Archaic, generally meaning the gifts given to a bride at the time of her marriage

2. Which poetic device is most apparent in line 7, "Of bending sky and sudden, sweeping showers"?

   (A) alliteration

   (B) assonance

   (C) annotation

   (D) elegy

   (E) syntax

3. The antecedent for the pronoun "he" in the phrase "he woos thee" (line 5) is

   (A) herald

   (B) sun

   (C) earth

   (D) flowers

   (E) ring

4. Which of the following is used figuratively?

   (A) "yellow trumpeter" (line 1)

   (B) "rich, brown earth" (line 5)

   (C) "gust of wind" (line 10)

   (D) "of April's sun" (line 13)

   (E) "joy untold" (line 9)

5. The primary metaphor in this poem is best said to express which of the following ideas?

   (A) courtship and marriage

   (B) the natural life of a flower

   (C) the effect of weather on plants

   (D) appreciation for a beautiful flower

   (E) the joy a flower brings to people's hearts

Questions 6–11. Read the following passage carefully before you choose your answers.

Line

It must not be thought that anyone could have mistaken [Carrie] for a nervous, sensitive, high-strung nature, cast unduly upon a cold, calculating, and unpoetic world. Such certainly she was not. But women are peculiarly sensitive to the personal adornment or equipment of their
(5) person, even the dullest, and particularly is this true of the young. Your bright-eyed, rosy-cheeked maiden, over whom a poet might well rave for the flowerlike expression of her countenance and the lissome and dainty grace of her body, may reasonably be dead to every evidence of the artistic and poetic in the unrelated evidences of life, and yet not lack in mate-
(10) rial appreciation. Never, it might be said, does she fail in this. With her the bloom of a rose may pass unappreciated, but the bloom of a fold of silk, never. The glint of a buckle, the hue of a precious stone, the faintest tints of the watered silk, these she would divine and qualify as readily as your poet if not more so. The creak, the rustle, the glow—the least and the
(15) best of the graven or spun—, these she would perceive and appreciate—if not because of some fashionable or hearsay quality, then on account of their true beauty, their innate fitness in any order of harmony, their place in the magical order and sequence of dress.

from the novel *Sister Carrie (1900)* by Theodore Dreiser

6. Carrie is being compared with

(A) a shop girl

(B) a poet

(C) a maiden

(D) a painter

(E) a dancer

7. The phrase "may reasonably be dead to" (line 8) is best interpreted to mean

(A) to be grieved by

(B) to be immune to

(C) to be apathetic toward

(D) to be enthralled with

(E) to be unaware of

8. "Even the dullest" (line 5) refers to

    (A) a flower bloom

    (B) a poet

    (C) a bolt of silk fabric

    (D) human nature

    (E) women

9. Which of the following best represents the author's purpose in this passage?

    (A) Define Carrie's ability to perceive the fitness and quality of material goods.

    (B) Show how young women are not intelligent.

    (C) Suggest that Carrie's abilities are akin to a poet's ability to perceive beauty in nature.

    (D) Illustrate the poet's role, even regarding trivial matters like material goods.

    (E) Describe a young woman, new to the fashion field.

10. Which of the following best describes the author's style in this passage?

    (A) ornate

    (B) imagistic

    (C) didactic

    (D) colloquial

    (E) reverent

11. The primary rhetorical strategy used in this passage is

    (A) exemplification

    (B) juxtaposition

    (C) classical argument

    (D) analogy

    (E) parody

Questions 12–18. Read the following poem carefully before you choose your answers.

A Solar Eclipse

Line

In that great journey of the stars through space
About the mighty, all-directing Sun,
The pallid, faithful Moon, has been the one
Companion of the Earth. Her tender face,
(5) Pale with the swift, keen purpose of that race,
Which at Time's natal hour was first begun,
Shines ever on her lover as they run
And lights his orbit with her silvery smile.
Sometimes such passionate love doth in her rise,
(10) Down from her beaten path she softly slips,
And with her mantle veils the Sun's bold eyes,
Then in the gloaming² finds her lover's lips.
While far and near the men our world call wise
See only that the Sun is in eclipse.

by Ella Wheeler Wilcox

12. The purpose of lines 4–7, "Her tender face, Pale with the swift, keen purpose of that race, Which at Time's natal hour was first begun, Shines ever on her lover as they run," is to

   (A) contrast with the Sun's dominance

   (B) illustrate how weak the Moon is

   (C) make clear that the Moon moves quickly

   (D) reinforce that the Moon has been constant since the beginning of time

   (E) emphasize how pale the Moon is

13. The Moon is in love with

   (A) time

   (B) the Sun

   (C) space

   (D) the Earth

   (E) the eclipse

---

² Twilight, dusk

14. According to the speaker, the world's wise men

    (A) seek objective knowledge of the solar system

    (B) treat the Moon unfairly because "she" is female

    (C) cannot fathom the mysteries of a solar eclipse

    (D) understand the origins of the Earth by studying solar events

    (E) give the Sun credit for its own eclipse

15. The primary literary device the poet uses in this poem is

    (A) personification

    (B) apostrophe

    (C) hyperbole

    (D) ironic juxtaposition

    (E) alliteration

16. The subject of the verb "shines" in line 7 is

    (A) face

    (B) time

    (C) race

    (D) Moon

    (E) lover

17. In Wheeler's poem, the Earth is characterized as male. The primary purpose of doing so is

    (A) to emphasize the Earth's natural masculine qualities

    (B) to lift up the Moon's feminine qualities, in contrast

    (C) to provide traditional gender roles for a romantic relationship

    (D) to suggest that the Earth is a more dominant celestial being

    (E) to make the Sun even more jealous

18. The phrase "beaten path" (line 10) is best understood as

(A) a symbol for life's hardships

(B) a metaphor for the Moon's orbit

(C) an ironic expression of the Moon's shyness

(D) a hyperbolic reference to the Moon's age

(E) a point of reference to show distance

Questions 19–25. Read the following passage carefully before you choose your answers.

Line

". . . All I desire is fame," wrote Margaret Cavendish, Duchess of Newcastle. And while she lived her wish was granted. Garish in her dress, eccentric in her habits, chaste in her conduct, coarse in her speech, she succeeded during her lifetime in drawing upon herself the ridicule of the

(5) great and the applause of the learned. But the last echoes of that clamour have now all died away; she lives only in the few splendid phrases that Lamb scattered upon her tomb; her poems, her plays, her philosophies, her orations, her discourses—all those folios and quartos in which, she protested, her real life was shrined—moulder in the gloom of public

(10) libraries, or are decanted into tiny thimbles which hold six drops of their profusion. Even the curious student, inspired by the words of Lamb, quails before the mass of her mausoleum, peers in, looks about him, and hurries out again, shutting the door.

But that hasty glance has shown him the outlines of a memorable fig-

(15) ure. Born (it is conjectured) in 1624, Margaret was the youngest child of a Thomas Lucas, who died when she was an infant, and her upbringing was due to her mother, a lady of remarkable character, of majestic grandeur and beauty "beyond the ruin of time." "She was very skillful in leases, and setting of lands and court keeping, ordering of stewards, and the like af-

(20) fairs." The wealth which thus accrued she spent, not on marriage portions, but on generous and delightful pleasures, "out of an opinion that if she bred us with needy necessity it might chance to create in us sharking quali- ties." Her eight sons and daughters were never beaten, but reasoned with, finely and gaily dressed, and allowed no conversation with servants, not

(25) because they are servants but because servants "are for the most part ill- bred as well as meanly born." The daughters were taught the usual accom- plishments "rather for formality than for benefit," it being their mother's opinion that character, happiness, and honesty were of greater value to a woman than fiddling and singing, or "the prating of several languages."

(30)   Already Margaret was eager to take advantage of such indulgence to gratify certain tastes. Already she liked reading better than needlework, dressing and "inventing fashions" better than reading, and writing best of all. Sixteen paper books of no title, written in straggling letters, for the impetuosity of her thought always outdid the pace of her fingers, testify to

(35)   the use she made of her mother's liberality. The happiness of their home life had other results as well. They were a devoted family. Long after they were married, Margaret noted, these handsome brothers and sisters, with their well-proportioned bodies, their clear complexions, brown hair, sound teeth, "tunable voices," and plain way of speaking, kept themselves "in a

(40)   flock together." The presence of strangers silenced them. But when they were alone, whether they walked in Spring Gardens or Hyde Park, or had music, or supped in barges upon the water, their tongues were loosed and they made "very merry amongst themselves, . . . judging, condemning, approving, commending, as they thought good."

(45)   The happy family life had its effect upon Margaret's character. As a child, she would walk for hours alone, musing and contemplating and reasoning with herself of "everything her senses did present." She took no pleasure in activity of any kind. Toys did not amuse her, and she could neither learn foreign languages nor dress as other people did. Her great pleasure was to in-

(50)   vent dresses for herself, which nobody else was to copy, "for," she remarks, "I always took delight in a singularity, even in accoutrements of habits."

Such a training, at once so cloistered and so free, should have bred a lettered old maid, glad of her seclusion, and the writer perhaps of some volume of letters or translations from the classics, which we should still

(55)   quote as proof of the cultivation of our ancestresses. But there was a wild streak in Margaret, a love of finery and extravagance and fame, which was for ever upsetting the orderly arrangements of nature.

from *The Duchess of Newcastle* by Virginia Woolf

19. Wolff's primary purpose in this excerpt is to

   (A) suggest the duchess had an easy childhood

   (B) point out that the duchess was a woman of her time

   (C) detail unfair gender roles in the 17th century

   (D) characterize a famous but forgotten writer's early life

   (E) illustrate that a woman can manage an estate as well as a man

20. Lamb, most likely, is

    (A) an admiring peer of Cavendish

    (B) the Duke of Newcastle

    (C) a tombstone engraver

    (D) an interested but timid student

    (E) one of Cavendish's teachers

21. The author's tone can best be described as

    (A) humorous

    (B) cynical

    (C) obsequious

    (D) envious

    (E) informative

22. "The orderly arrangements of nature" (line 57) can best be interpreted to mean

    (A) the natural growth of children, despite which class they're born into

    (B) society's defined gender roles and expectations for the sexes

    (C) the impact of fame on the duchess

    (D) an acknowledgement that women were not meant to be writers

    (E) a reference to how fitting it was that in the end Margaret became an "old maid, glad of her seclusion" (line 53)

23. The author's use of quoted material throughout the passage serves to

    (A) provide added credibility to the facts in her biographical account

    (B) show an alternative view of life in the 17th century

    (C) add imagery and figurative language to an otherwise expository work

    (D) discount the duchess's own view of her life

    (E) to showcase Cavendish's talent as a writer

24. Cavendish's mother's attitude towards teaching her daughters "the usual accomplishments" (lines 26–27) reveals

    (A) how much she values and maintains traditional female social roles

    (B) her obvious preference for her male heirs

    (C) she cares more for their personal well-being than teaching what society expects

    (D) her refusal to consider a more modern view of educating women

    (E) she values her male and female children as equals

25. The final paragraph in this passage serves to

    (A) minimize the influence Cavendish had on women writers who followed

    (B) prove that Cavendish was not much of a notable writer after all

    (C) reinforce the fact that women were not respected as writers

    (D) inspire Wolff, herself a woman who broke away from societal conventions

    (E) illustrate that Cavendish enjoyed a life of quiet seclusion

ANSWERS AND EXPLANATIONS

1. (C)   The correct response is apostrophe (C), which is when a speaker addresses something that cannot respond, generally something non-living or non-human. An ode is a particular form of poetry, wherein the speaker addresses an object or a subject. However, an ode is a form, not a device. There is no evidence in the title to support any of the other choices.

2. (A)   Alliteration is the repetition of beginning sounds, clearly evident in line 7. "Assonance" (B) refers to the repetition of vowel sounds, which is not evident in the line. "Annotation" (C) is not a poetic device but a method of marking a text for deep, critical reading. "Syntax" (E) simply means the arrangement of words in a line, but it is not necessarily a poetic device on its own. And "elegy" (D) is a type of poem meant to reflect on the death of a subject, not a poetic device.

3. (B)   In finding this pronoun's antecedent ask, "who or what woos?" Also, eliminate as a choice a noun found in a preceding prepositional phrase. Prepositional phrases, while they are informative, are grammatically inert. Ring (E) and earth (C) are both found in prepositional phrases, so they can be quickly eliminated. Flowers (D) is plural not singular. Herald (A) is clearly an appellation given to the subject of this poem.

4. (A)   The poet likely sees a similarity in shape between a daffodil and a trumpet, so "yellow trumpeter" is clearly a metaphor. Connotatively, a trumpet is the instrument of a herald, so the metaphor works on more than one level. "Rich, brown earth" (B) is simple imagery, as is (C) a "gust of wind." "April's sun" (D) is only a detail letting readers know the time of year. "Joy untold" (E) does seem to be somewhat hyperbolic, but it is a much weaker example of figurative language than response (A).

5. (A)   While the poem does depict a flower's life (B) as well as suggest that warm earth and spring rain help the plant grow (C), neither aspect is figurative. Nor is the sense that a beautiful flower brings joy (E). While the reader of this poem might feel appreciation for a beautiful flower (D), the poet does not present figurative language to that effect. The only correct answer is courtship and marriage (A). Lowell tells us the sun "woos" the daffodil. A dowry (used in its archaic form here as 'dowers' to satisfy the rhyme scheme) is, in particular, a wedding gift. The use of the words "jewelled" and "gold" are suggestive of a wedding ring, particularly "gold" as in the end, the flower catches the ring or "wears" it.

6. (B)   While one can infer Carrie would be well suited to work in a dress shop (A), there is no evidence in this excerpt to support that particular choice. While Carrie is likely "a maiden" (C), since the author implies she is young, it is Dreiser's comparison of Carrie to a poet that is most prominent in his characterization. As evidence, he says Carrie stands in contrast to those who lack the ability to see "the artistic and poetic." Further evidence is found in lines 10–14. And while "a painter" (D) and "a dancer" (E) are both artists, there is no direct evidence for either of those choices.

7. (E)   Dead suggests lifelessness, so strong emotion such as "grieved" or "enthralled" are contradictory. While apathy indicates a lack of interest, it's still a chosen or active emotion. To be immune to means to be pro-

tected from, but there is no evidence the young women have any barrier to their experience. The only logical answer is (E), to be unaware.

8. (E)   Grammatically the adjective "dullest" (line 5) can only refer to a woman, even though the antecedent is "women" (line 3). Look for antecedent parts of speech in the same sentence. While this "rule" is not always a perfect guide, it is a good idea to remember it.

9. (C)   Carrie's ability to determine a fine quality silk, among other things, is part of Dreiser's point: she is like a poet in her highly refined sensibilities, so the correct response is (C). Answer (A) involves the opposite assessment of Carrie's abilities. While the author does say some young women are "dull" (B), the passage doesn't dwell on that idea. Nor does Dreiser give more than a subtle hint that Carrie is new to the world of women's apparel (E). The best evidence for (C) is found in lines 10–14.

10. (B)   While the syntax in this excerpt is sophisticated, the passage is direct and relatively succinct. No hyperbolic language is apparent, so ornate (A) would not be a logical choice. The writer is also not attempting to teach or instruct (C). Throughout, idioms or customs of speech that indicate a colloquial style are missing. While the writer seems to appreciate Carrie's sensibilities, there's no evidence he reveres her (E). Phrases like "bright eyed, rosy cheeked" and "faintest tints of silk" reinforce the imagistic style (B).

11. (A)   Particularly in lines 11–14, Dreiser gives examples to support his assertions, but not just there. He illustrates by example throughout the passage. (A), exemplification, is the correct answer. A classical argument (C) would require particular parts, introduction, confirmation, concession, etc. There is no evidence of an opposite or contrasting element that could serve in juxtaposition, so (B) is incorrect. Use of analogy would require a parallel story used to emphasize the main narrative. There isn't one, so (D) is incorrect. Lastly, elements of parody, (E), such as exaggeration or other forms of satire, are not present.

12. (D)   "Time's natal hour" means time's first hour, so when the poet follows that statement with "ever on," she is reinforcing the moon's constancy over all of time. There is nothing in these lines regarding the Sun's dominance (A). Constancy is not a weakness, so (B) is incorrect. While the word "swift" (C) indicates speed, the moon's prompt attention to the Sun is not the primary focus of these lines.

(E) The Moon's pale face is an inherent quality of the Moon, used descriptively, but doesn't dominate the poet's purpose in these lines.

13. (D) "The Earth" is the only logical choice. The poet characterizes the moon's relationship with the Earth, and says the Moon is a "faithful companion." Further evidence can be found in the second stanza when the moon "veils" the Sun's bold eyes, allowing her to sneak a kiss.

14. (E) Not until the end of the poem does the poet mention the Earth's wise men. While it is ironic that such wise men disregard the role the Moon plays in a solar eclipse, there is no evidence to support answers other than (E). The men see only the effect of the Moon, and not the Moon, herself.

15. (A) The poet gives the Moon human qualities throughout the poem, most effectively in line 12, when she says the Moon "finds her lover's lips." No other response is logical.

16. (A) In looking for antecedents of verbs, the best practice is to ask "who or what" in terms of the verb and look backwards. In this case, ask "who or what shines?" Antecedents will also be fairly close in proximity. What shines in this poem is the Moon's "face."

17. (C) The Earth is literally neither male nor female (A), but the poet personifies the Moon as female, so logically the Moon's lover would be male, so (C) is correct. There is no evidence for the other answers.

18. (B) While we sometimes refer to life as a path, and to be beaten means to be worn down, in this poem, the metaphor "beaten path" clearly refers to an orbit.

19. (D) The only correct answer is (D), even though there is evidence in the excerpt for the ideas in the other choices. The key to choosing correctly here is that you're asked for the "primary," or main purpose.

20. (A) An admiring peer would have an opinion and it's logical he would have been asked to provide a fitting epitaph. We know Lamb is famous, since Wolff refers to him only by his last name. If he were the Duke of Newcastle (B), his last name would be Cavendish. Tombstone engravers (C) would have been common laborers and not asked to provide epitaphs. The student (D) is not an actual person, but a hypothetical example of one who might take a glancing interest in Cavendish's grave.

You can rule out (E), one of Cavendish's teachers, since this excerpt implies much of Cavendish's education came through her mother.

21. **(E)** Determining tone requires an assessment of the author's attitude. In this case, Woolf primarily hopes to inform. She is not cynical (B) in her assessment of Cavendish, nor does she praise her subject to an obsequious (C) extent. While it's clear Woolf admires Cavendish, no evidence exists to suggest she's envious (D). Throughout, nothing suggests a humorous intent (A). Even if (E) were not your first choice, you could find the correct response by process of elimination.

22. **(B)** The best interpretation is (B), society's expectations or sense of what is orderly or correct for men or women. Children, who grow naturally (A), may defy social expectations. The impact of fame (C) on Cavendish was only one way she upset this "orderly arrangement." There is no evidence for choices (D) or (E), but the selection of either one may indicate a superficial reading of the text.

23. **(A)** While the quoted material does add vivid detail, it is not more imagistic or figurative (C) than the rest of the passage. The quoted material does not provide a contrasting view of life (B) nor does it minimize or discount the duchess's view of life (D). While the quoted material was written by Cavendish (E), the author uses it to support her claims and illustrate her main ideas (A) and not to praise the duchess.

24. **(C)** Cavendish says her mother thought "character, happiness, and honesty were of greater value to a woman than fiddling and singing, or 'the prating of several languages'"(lines 29). There's no evidence in the passage that the children's mother gave preferential treatment to the boys, and while she seemed conscious of the need to support her daughters' independence (a modern view), she did nothing to diminish the boys as a result. The children are reported to have grown up well and strong.

25. **(D)** Clearly Woolf admires the subject of her work, so she had no intent to minimize Cavendish (A). Woolf laments that Cavendish's works "moulder in the gloom of public libraries," so (B) cannot be correct. In her time, Cavendish was respected, in particular by Lamb (C). Clearly (E) is incorrect, as Cavendish is shown to be a vivacious character. The only conclusion is that Cavendish's refusal to bow to society's expectations, both as a child and as an adult is something that Woolf admires.